—— MBA ——
ECONOMICS

To Ethel B. Jones and Richard H. Timberlake, Jr.,
Mentors and friends

—— MBA ——
ECONOMICS

Mark Jackson

San Jose State University

First published 1996

Blackwell Publishers, a publishing imprint of
Basil Blackwell, Inc.
238 Main Street
Cambridge, Massachusetts 02142
USA

Basil Blackwell Ltd.
108 Cowley Road
Oxford OX4 1JF
UK

Library of Congress Cataloging-in-Publication Data
Jackson, Mark, 1937–
    MBA economics / Mark Jackson.
        p.   cm.
    Includes index.
    ISBN 1-55786-631-7
    1. Economics.   2. Microeconomics.   I. Title.
    HB171.5.J232   1996
    330—dc20   94-46727
                                                                    CIP

British Library Cataloguing in Publication Data
A CIP catalogue record for this book is available from the British Library.

Typeset by Cornerstone Composition Services.
Printed in the USA by Book Crafters.
This book is printed on acid free paper.

Contents

To Instructors

Each year tens of thousands of individuals enroll in MBA programs, executive MBA programs, six-week business school courses, and other courses of study in which they are required to come up to speed quickly in economics. This text presents these students with an intensive first course in microeconomics.

Economists assume that all individuals pursue their own interests through their actions. Accordingly, rather than merely presenting economics to students, I present economics within the context of arguments addressed to their self-interest. Thus, only the economics necessary to support the arguments need be presented. This feature makes possible a text substantially leaner than the standard text in microeconomics. At the same time, this brevity in exposition makes possible a more comprehensive discussion of factor markets than is usual in a micro text.

THE PARTICULAR ARGUMENTS OF THIS TEXT

Part I presents some familiar conclusions from the product market. The first overarching conclusion that students reach is that goods and services tend to be produced *efficiently* in purely competitive product markets.

> *(1) In purely competitive product markets, prices tend toward minimum long-run average total costs of production. (Chapters 2–5)*

This argument begins in Chapter 2 and continues through Chapters 3, 4, and 5. In Chapter 2, students construct the theory of consumer choice and find that product demand is a conclusion of that theory. This chapter also treats the topics of elasticity of demand and market demand. In Chapter 3, students construct the theory of producer choice and find that product supply is a conclusion of that theory. Elasticity of supply and market supply are also

presented here. In Chapter 4, students examine the determinants of equilibrium price and quantity of a good and encounter those factors that cause
equilibrium price and quantity to change. After an initial discussion of
long-run costs in Chapter 5, students reach the conclusion that product price
tends toward minimum long-run average total costs in purely competitive
product markets.

The conclusion that purely competitive product markets inexorably produce efficient outcomes has a major implication for consumer welfare. Given
an individual's money income, her real income (thus her consumption and
utility) will be higher, the lower the prices of the goods and services she
consumes. This set of chapters argues that these prices will tend toward their
minimum in the long run in purely competitive product markets. Thus, the
self-interest-seeking activities of producers harnessed by means of exchange
within purely competitive product markets inadvertently benefit consumers.
Students learn a great deal of economics in these four chapters, but they learn
economics in order to understand an argument addressed to their self-interest.

*(2) Activities of self-interest-seeking producers can cause the conclusions of
the purely competitive model to be altered in their favor. (Chapter 6)*

The purely competitive model is a limit-case model. In this chapter, the
limit-case model of monopoly is presented. Students learn exactly how they
become worse off as a consequence of the most severe limitations on their
options for choice in the product market. They also examine rent-seeking
activities of producers that are designed to protect their profits and that, if
successful, generate an element of rent in product prices.

The economics of factor markets is the subject of Part II. Given the prices
of the goods and services that an individual consumes, her real income (thus
her consumption and utility) will be higher, when her money income is
higher. One determinant of her annual money income is the wage at which
she can work, given her skills. The first argument in the labor market is that
there are inexorable tendencies toward *equality of wages* for like types of labor
in purely competitive labor markets.

*(3) Average real wages for like types of labor will tend toward equality
across both industries and regions in purely competitive labor markets.
(Chapters 7–10)*

This overarching argument in the labor market spans four chapters. In
Chapter 7, students construct the theory of producer choice again and find
that labor demand is a conclusion of that theory. They learn that the wage
workers receive tends to be the maximum that the firm is willing to pay: the

VMPP of workers. They construct the theory of consumer choice again in Chapter 8 and see that labor supply (where the quantity variable is hours supplied) is a conclusion of that theory. The labor force participation decision is also presented as a function of the wage rate. Chapter 9 presents a model of equilibrium occupational wage and employment determination and discusses the factors that cause equilibrium wages and employment to change. In Chapter 10, students examine those equilibrating mechanisms that tend, in the long run, to generate *equality of wages* for like types of labor across both industries and regions in purely competitive labor markets.

(4) Through rent-seeking activities, occupational groups may be able to generate an element of rent in their occupational wage. (Chapter 11)

Chapter 11 presents the model of monopsony and shows that workers will be exploited if the labor market is characterized by monopsony. Furthermore, occupational groups also engage in rent-seeking activity by limiting entry into occupations. Occupational wages will contain an element of rent if this activity succeeds.

Throughout the discussion of the labor market, the individual's skills are taken as given. Chapter 12 concludes the presentation of factor markets with a discussion of capital theory. Individuals can make human-capital investments in themselves, permitting their entry into higher-paying occupations. Similarly, firms make human-capital investments in their workers in the form of on-the-job training.

(5) Human-capital investments in individuals can increase the wage at which they can work. (Chapter 12)

A SUCCESSFUL TIME FRAME

All of these arguments can be presented in one term. It will be necessary, however, to keep an eye on the calendar so that you are completing the product market arguments at or around midterm.

1

Introduction

Each of the individual sciences is a logically articulated structure of falsifiable opinions about nature. In any science, the structure of these opinions is identical: "If A, then Z." In this structure A is the hypothesis and Z is the conclusion. Because all sciences begin with a hypothesis, it seems fitting to begin this presentation by introducing the hypothesis of economics.

1.1 THE SELF-INTEREST-SEEKING INDIVIDUAL

Each of the individual sciences marks off a portion of the universe for its own special study. Economists mark off human behavior for their special study.

Simple observation permits you to see that humans do all sorts of things: they get married; they have children; they murder their neighbors; they go on vacations; they allow themselves to be shot to the moon. These are behaviors that you can perceive simply by opening your eyes and ears. But there is another portion of reality as well, an underlying principle in invisible nature that gives rise to the behaviors that you see. Because this underlying principle cannot be seen, it must be imagined. Since first enunciated more than two centuries ago by Adam Smith, economists assume that self-interest is the underlying principle that gives rise to the human behavior we see. Thus, the hypothesis that underlies the economist's theory of human behavior is that individuals pursue their own interests through their actions.

Many individuals will immediately conclude that the public welfare must be adversely affected if individuals pursue their own interests through their actions. Economists, however, propose a different argument. We explain how individual self-interest can be harnessed in such a way that it promotes the interests of the larger society as well.

1

Exchange as a Means to Ends   Self-interest is an assumed end, goal, or objective. Self-interest-seeking individuals in any society confront a small number of potential means to their ends. They can, for example, rely on others, hoping that their own needs will be attended to by the benevolent actions of friends. Another potential means that individuals can employ is coercion, taking from others by force or fraud the goods that satisfy their needs. Economists examine the consequences of self-interest-seeking individuals pursuing their objectives in society by means of exchange.

To cooperate is to work together with others in society. This concept is almost always understood by the public to mean working together with others to attain a common objective. But cooperation has another meaning as well: working together with others in order to pursue individual (and differing) objectives. Exchange is human cooperation in this second sense.

Each party to an exchange has his individual objectives that he attempts to attain as a result of exchange. When individuals cooperate with others by means of exchange, each party gives something; but the giving is not a gift because each party receives something in exchange for the giving. (If you give with no expectation of receiving anything in exchange, then your giving is a gift.) Exchange, then, is a form of human cooperation in which each party receives as well as gives. Do not imagine that exchanges are only formal proposals that occur infrequently in society; when you return a smile and a hello, you have participated in an exchange.

All exchanges are voluntary. A self-interest-seeking individual will voluntarily give up something in an exchange only if he values what he receives more than he values what he gives up. For exchange to be possible, then, it is necessary that individuals differ in the subjective valuations they place on things in the world. Because individuals do differ in this characteristic, a self-interest-seeking individual can pursue his individual objectives by means of exchange.

There are those in society who believe that the general welfare is promoted only when one gives to his neighbor. In the opinion of economists, giving does produce positive-sum outcomes in society; when one gives to his neighbor, the giver satisfies a need by giving, and the recipient of the gift benefits as well. But because parties to an exchange gain more than they lose, there are also positive-sum outcomes in society when self-interest-seeking individuals pursue their objectives in society through exchange. Thus, there are two activities in any society that produce positive-sum outcomes: giving and exchange.

The truth that there are net benefits to each participant in exchange has led some to characterize exchange as a "positive-sum game." If one employs the metaphor of human life as a game, then living is playing the game called life. All games are played according to rules. Using these metaphors, exchange is a rule, not a game. If self-interest-seeking individuals play the game of life (live) by this rule, their self-interest-seeking choices do unintentionally benefit others in society. There are positive-sum outcomes in society when individuals abide by the rule of exchange in living.

Purely Competitive Markets When self-interest-seeking individuals pursue their objectives in society by means of exchange, their chances of attaining those objectives are greater when the array of options in exchange is greater. In the real world, individuals confront a variety of options in exchange, ranging from many to few. Economists have intentionally constructed a limit-case model in which individuals confront the widest possible array of options in exchange. This construction is the purely competitive model. Thus, in purely competitive labor markets, individuals with the skills necessary to enter an occupation confront the widest possible array of options in exchange – all those employers who employ those skills. Furthermore, if an individual chooses to increase his skills so as to enter a higher paying occupation, no artificial barriers prevent him from doing so. Similarly, individuals in purely competitive product markets confront the widest possible array of options in consumption. And if new producers choose to enter an industry and increase the options for consumers, no artificial barriers prevent their doing so.

If self-interest-seeking individuals pursue their own objectives by means of exchange in purely competitive markets, will there be a resulting order in society, or will society be characterized by chaos? Answering this central question requires knowledge of economics.

1.2 ECONOMICS: A LOGICALLY ARTICULATED STRUCTURE OF FALSIFIABLE OPINIONS ABOUT NATURE

Because each science begins with a hypothesis, each science begins with an imaginative statement. But this hypothesis in turn marks the beginning of a process of construction, for each science is a structure. Furthermore, each science is a logically articulated structure: any conclusion Z in any science must follow logically from the hypothesis. Thus, constructing science requires both imagination and reason. Consider now the reasoning from "if A" to "then Z" in economics.

Economics: A Logically Articulated Structure An important part of the effort of economic inquiry is generating logically articulated conclusions about human behavior. For example, "if" individual consumers pursue their own interests through their actions, "then" a change in the price of a good will lead them to change their consumption of the good in the opposite direction. (This logical conclusion has a name in economics: product demand.) Similarly, "if" individual producers pursue their own interests through their actions, "then" a change in the price of their output will lead them to change the production of that output in the same direction. (This logical conclusion also has a name in economics: product supply.) For more than two centuries economists have been fully employed forging just such links between the hypothesis of the self-interest-seeking individual and a variety of behavioral conclusions that follow logically from the hypothesis. Furthermore, this inventory of logical inferences continues to grow as economists extend their analysis into more and more areas of human behavior.

Economics: A Logically Articulated Structure of Falsifiable Opinions

The final objective of all scientific inquiry is knowledge of nature's world. Because nature's world is external to and independent of each individual, scientific inquiry cannot be merely a self-contained mental activity of reasoning from hypothesis to conclusion, with no care or concern for nature's world. It is at this point that the role of evidence presents itself for consideration. The role of evidence in scientific inquiry is clear: evidence either supports or fails to support the conclusions of science. Although some may wish to use evidence to call into doubt the hypotheses of scientific theories, in scientific inquiry evidence is produced either to support or to attack the conclusions that follow from those hypotheses. Thus, all scientific statements must have the potential to be falsified by evidence.

In turn, because scientific statements must have the potential to be falsified by evidence, such statements are necessarily opinions, not beliefs. Both opinions and beliefs have a common characteristic: they are both ideas that people hold. But beliefs are ideas that people hold immune from evidence, ideas that they hold on faith. By contrast, individuals are willing to consider changing their opinions on the basis of evidence.

1.3 WHAT IS SCIENTIFIC KNOWLEDGE FOR?

Although the objective of scientific inquiry is knowledge of nature's world, the scientific knowledge produced over the centuries by scientific inquiry is in turn a means to a further and final end. Jacob Bronowski writes that scientists extract from the universe its own harmonies "for our good." Economists agree entirely. Knowledge of nature is for *our* sake, not "for its own sake."

Because all scientific knowledge is ultimately for our good, the microeconomics in this text is presented within the context of arguments addressed to your self-interest. Thus, as you progress through this work, it will be made clear that the economics you are learning is not merely "for its own sake" but for *your* sake.

PART
——— I ———

Pure Competition and Efficiency:
Product Markets

In purely competitive product markets, the prices individuals pay for the various goods and services they consume will tend, in the long run, toward the minimum per-unit total costs of producing them. In other words, purely competitive product markets tend to produce *efficient* outcomes. This overarching argument is the first of two major arguments in Part I.

Product demand is one necessary element of this argument. In Chapter 2, we construct the theory of consumer choice and find that product demand is a conclusion of that theory. Product supply is also a necessary part of this argument. In Chapter 3, we construct the theory of producer choice and find that product supply is a conclusion of that theory. Chapter 4 presents a model of product–price determination and examines those factors that cause product price to change. In Chapter 5, we reach the following overarching conclusion regarding purely competitive product markets: product prices tend, in the long run, toward the minimum per-unit total costs of production.

Real income is the purchasing power of your money income. Given your money income, any decrease in the prices of the goods and services you consume will increase your real income. Increases in your real income allow you to increase your consumption of goods and services. Because product prices tend toward the minimum per-unit total costs of production in the long run in purely competitive markets, your consumption tends toward its maximum in such markets.

There is a second related argument in Part I: the self-interest-seeking activities of producers may be able to prevent this long-run movement of product price toward minimum per-unit total costs, thus maintaining their product price (and profits). In Chapter 6, we discover how producers can maintain their profits at the expense of consumers.

———— 2 ————

Product Demand: A Conclusion of the Theory of Consumer Choice

In this chapter, we construct the theory of consumer choice. Beginning from the hypothesis of the self-interest-seeking individual, we proceed step-by-step to a logical conclusion of that theory: product demand. Before setting off on this journey, however, it is important to have a clear notion of our destination.

2.1 PRODUCT DEMAND DEFINED

An individual's demand for any good X is a relation between two variables: the price of X and the quantity demanded of X. In this relation, the dependent variable is the quantity demanded of X; the price of X is the independent variable. Furthermore, the demand for X is a negative relation between these two variables: any change in the price of X will lead an individual to change the quantity demanded of X in the opposite direction. Figure 2.1 illustrates an individual's demand for X.

The demand for X can be interpreted in two different ways, both of which are equally valid. In one interpretation, the demand for X is a series of "if, then" statements. Thus, *if* the price of X in Figure 2.1 were P, *then* the quantity demanded of X would be Q. *If* the price of X were P*, *then* the quantity demanded of X would be Q*.

It is also correct to say that demand illustrates the maximum price that an individual will be willing to pay for various quantities of X. Thus, the maximum price that this individual is willing to pay for the quantity Q is the price P. The maximum price that this individual is willing to pay for the quantity Q* is the price P*.

9

The demand for X is a conclusion of the theory of consumer choice. Your first task in this chapter is to reproduce a theory that enables you to conclude that a self-interest-seeking individual will change the consumption of any good X in a direction opposite from the change in the price of X. To economists, this conclusion is of enormous generality and importance in understanding human behavior.

2.2 INDIFFERENCE CURVES

The theory of consumer choice begins with a hypothesis: the individual is pursuing her own interests through her actions. In particular, economists assume in this theory that the individual attempts to maximize her own total utility through her actions. This assumption immediately raises a question: what is utility?

Needs, Goods, and Utility   In order to discuss the concept of utility, it is necessary to introduce two other related concepts: needs and goods. Econo-

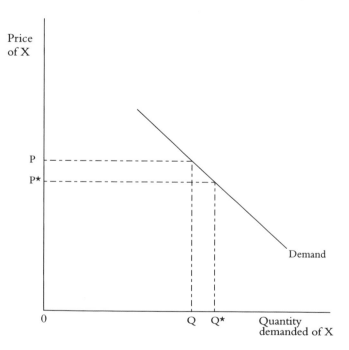

Figure 2.1   An individual's demand for X. The demand for X is a negative relation between the price of X (the independent variable) and the quantity demanded of X (the dependent variable).

mists assume first that all individuals have unsatisfied needs. We do not know if people have different needs, or if needs change over time. Economists assume simply that individuals have unsatisfied needs.

The universe consists of things. A fountain pen is a thing; marriage is a thing; an orange is a thing. If the consumption of some thing satisfies a need of an individual, then that thing is a good to the individual. Individuals differ as to which things in the universe they view as goods. To one individual, Super Bowl tickets and fast cars are goods; another individual receives no utility from consuming these things.

If individuals have unsatisfied needs, and if those needs are satisfied by the consumption of goods, what then is utility? Utility is the feeling of well-being (or relief from felt uneasiness) that results from the consumption of goods.

Indifference Curves   Figure 2.2 illustrates how total utility varies with the consumption of two goods. Quantities of good X are on the horizontal axis. Quantities of some other good Y are on the vertical axis. Combination A represents quantities of two goods: X_A of good X and Y_A of good Y. From consuming this combination of two goods, this individual receives some amount of total utility. If she consumed combination B, would her level of total utility be greater than from consuming combination A? Yes, because combination B contains the same quantity of good Y (Y_A) but more of good X (X_B). Because total utility varies directly with the consumption of goods, her level of total utility is clearly greater. Furthermore, she receives more total utility from consuming any combination in quadrant 1 than from consuming combination A. This is true because each combination in quadrant 1 contains either more of one good (and no less of the other) or more of both goods. Most combinations, of course, contain more of both goods. Thus, any combination in quadrant 1 is preferred to combination A.

What about combination C relative to A? Both combinations contain the same amount of good Y (Y_A), but combination C contains less of good X (X_C rather than X_A). Combination C, then, is inferior to A because the level of total utility in C is less. Furthermore, any combination in quadrant 3 yields less total utility than does combination A because each combination in quadrant 3 contains either less of one good (and no less of the other) or less of both goods. Most combinations, of course, contain less of both goods. Thus, combination A is preferred to any combination in quadrant 3.

This discussion leads, then, to a consideration of all those combinations that yield the individual the same amount of total utility as does combination A. These combinations will always contain more of one good but less of the other. These combinations will lie in quadrants 2 and 4 and can be connected by an indifference curve. An indifference curve, then, always has a negative slope and contains all those combinations of two goods that yield the same amount of total utility. It is because total utility is constant along an indifference curve that an individual is indifferent to the various combinations that lie on the curve. As far as she is concerned, the loss in total utility from consuming less of one good is exactly offset by the gain in total utility from consuming more of the other good. Thus, the slope of an indifference curve measures the rate at which the individual is willing to make substitutions in consumption, keeping total utility unchanged.

You saw earlier that individuals may differ from each other in those things in the universe they view as goods. Now you see that there is a second way in which individuals may differ from each other: two individuals may both view Super Bowl tickets as a good, but may differ in the rate at which they are willing

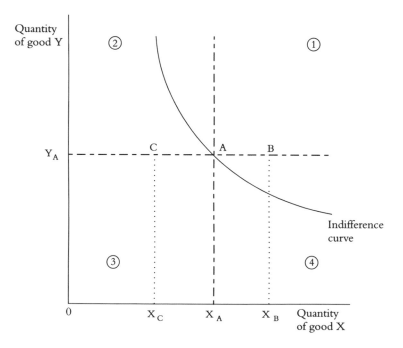

Figure 2.2   An indifference curve for an individual. The combinations of goods X and Y that provide this individual with the same total utility as combination A lie on an indifference curve that passes through quadrants 2 and 4. It is because total utility is the same for all combinations of two goods on this indifference curve that the individual is "indifferent" to these combinations.

to give up other goods to get those tickets. You could illustrate this difference by varying the slopes of the indifference curves for the two individuals.

This discussion of the total utility an individual receives from various combinations of two goods can readily be generalized. Will there be some combinations that yield the same amount of total utility as combination B? Yes, and all such combinations will lie on a negatively sloped indifference curve that passes through combination B. Whereas the individual is indifferent to any combination along the indifference curve passing through B, any of these combinations is preferred to any combination on the indifference curve passing through A. Why? Because the individual preferred combination B to combination A to begin with.

Figure 2.3 illustrates only three of many such indifference curves. This "family" of indifference curves represents some important characteristics of individuals. First, indifference curves are "everywhere dense." This means that every possible combination of the two goods will lie on some indifference curve. Second, indifference curves do not intersect. No individual will prefer

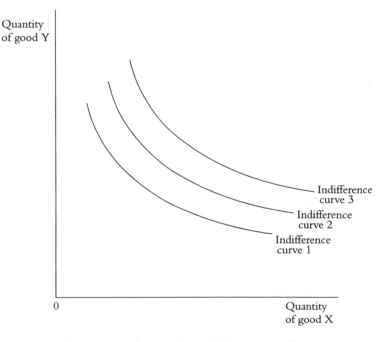

Figure 2.3   A "family" of indifference curves for an individual. Indifference curves have three important characteristics. First, they are "everywhere dense." Second, they are convex with respect to the origin. Third, they do not intersect.

a combination on a higher indifference curve to a combination on a lower indifference curve, yet simultaneously be indifferent to a combination that lies on both. Lastly, note that each indifference curve is not a straight line but rather convex with respect to the origin. If an indifference curve were a straight line, what would it represent about the individual? The slope of a straight line is constant. Thus, if an indifference curve were a straight line, it would indicate that an individual is willing to substitute one good for another at a constant rate, regardless of the quantities of each good she currently consumes. Economists argue that individuals are willing to substitute one good for another in consumption, but not at a constant rate. Why not?

Earlier you saw that individuals have unsatisfied needs and that they attempt to satisfy those needs by consuming goods. If some good (such as water) can satisfy a variety of needs, what needs will individuals satisfy first as they begin to consume the good? Economists assume that individuals satisfy their most urgent needs first. Because additional quantities of any good go to satisfy ever less urgent needs, individuals will be willing to give up ever smaller quantities of other goods to satisfy those less urgent needs. Thus, the slope of an indifference is convex with respect to the origin.

What is it that prevents individuals from satisfying all of their needs and thus achieving infinitely large levels of total utility in the real world? In terms of Figure 2.3, why do individuals not choose a combination on the highest indifference curve? The reason is that they are constrained. Thus, self-interest-seeking individuals attempt to maximize their own total utility subject to constraints.

2.3   INCOME CONSTRAINTS

What quantity of good X could an individual consume if she spent all of her income on that good? In Figure 2.4 that quantity is X. Alternately, what quantity of good Y could an individual consume if all of her income were spent on good Y? That quantity is Y. She can, of course, consume all other quantities that lie on or within the straight line YX. This straight line YX is this individual's real income constraint. To illustrate an increase in real income, shift the position of the income constraint to the right, parallel to itself.

But note that the real income constraint has not only a position but also a slope. What does the slope of an income constraint illustrate? The slope of the real income constraint is dY/dX and measures the rate at which one good can be substituted for the other. The rate at which goods can be substituted for each other is the relative price of the goods. The fact that the income constraint is a straight line illustrates that this relative price is assumed to be constant.

2.4 ONE PRICE, ONE QUANTITY

We began to construct the theory of consumer choice by assuming that an individual makes choices so as to maximize her total utility. We now know as a result of the discussion in Section 2.2 how to illustrate an individual's preferences. In Section 2.3 we learned how to illustrate the individual's real income constraint. We now have enough information to determine the quantity of X this individual will choose to consume given her preferences, her real income, and the price of X. Figure 2.5 illustrates this quantity that maximizes her total utility. Which combination of the two goods X and Y will this individual choose? The best combination is that which provides the highest amount of total utility – the combination lying on the highest attainable indifference curve. This is combination U in Figure 2.5, the combination

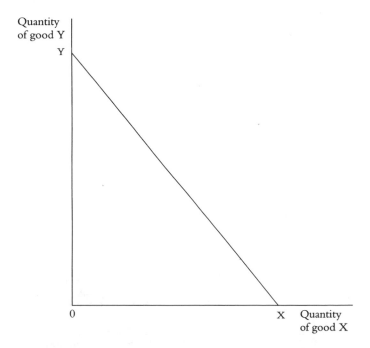

Figure 2.4 An income constraint for an individual. If this individual were to spend all of her income on good X, she could consume X of that good. Similarly, if she were to spend all of her income on good Y, she could consume Y of that good. Or, she could consume all combinations of goods X and Y that lie on YX, the real income constraint. The real income constraint also has a slope; it represents the rate at which one good can be substituted for another. The fact that this real income constraint is a straight line illlustrates that this rate is assumed to be constant.

for which the income constraint is tangent to (touches) indifference curve 2. Notice that combination T is attainable but is not chosen and that combination V is preferred to U but is not attainable. Given this individual's preferences, her real income, and the price of X, the utility-maximizing combination is U, the attainable combination for which total utility is at a maximum. Combination U contains X_U of good X.

Is the demand for X this particular quantity demanded of X at this particular price of X? No, it is not. Demand is a series of "if, then" statements. Here there is only one price of X and one quantity demanded of X. What you must now do to reach the conclusion of this theory is to change the price of X and see whether this utility-maximizing individual will change her consumption of X in the same direction or in the opposite direction from the change in the price of X. A theoretical statement is always a logical prediction about the expected direction of change of the dependent variable.

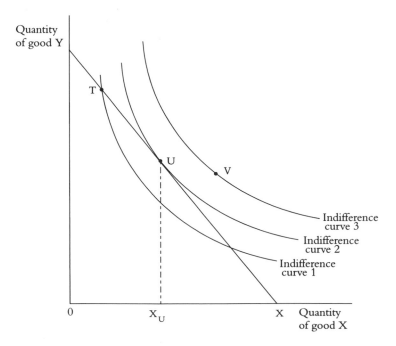

Figure 2.5   One price, one quantity. The attainable combination that yields the most total utility is combination U which lies on indifference curve 2. Combination U contains X_U of good X. Thus, given this individual's preferences, her real income, and the price of good X, she chooses to consume X_U of the good. This combination of price of X and quantity demanded of X represents one combination in the demand for X.

2.5 REACHING THE CONCLUSION

Figure 2.6 illustrates a fall in the price of good X. The income constraint has pivoted around pivot point Y and now intersects the horizontal axis at X^*. Now this individual's income will allow her to consume more (X^*) of good X if she spends all her income on that good. How is this possible? It is possible because the price of X has fallen.

Because of the fall in the price of X, this individual can now attain more combinations of the two goods than she could before. Which of the attainable combinations will she choose? As before, she will choose that attainable combination that yields the highest level of total utility. In Figure 2.6 that combination is now V. Combination V contains more of good X (X_V rather than X_U).

Figure 2.7 illustrates these two price–quantity combinations. If the price of X were P, then this individual would consume X of the good. If the price

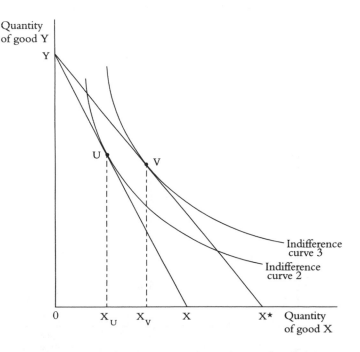

Figure 2.6 A fall in the price of good X. The pivoting of the real income constraint from YX to YX* represents a decrease in the price of X. As a result of the fall in the price of X, combination V is now the attainable combination that yields the highest amount of total utility. Combination V contains X_V of good X. Thus, as a result of the fall in the price of X, the individual increases her consumption of this good from X_U to X_V.

of X fell to P*, then she would increase her consumption of this good to X*. This negative relation between the price and quantity demanded of X is the destination that you set out to reach. You can now say that "if"an individual is assumed to be a utility maximizer, "then" she will change the quantity demanded of any good X in a direction opposite from the change in the price of the good.

2.6 INCOME AND RELATIVE PRICE EFFECTS OF A FALL IN THE PRICE OF X

When the price of X falls, the individual increases the consumption of X for two entirely different reasons. First, a fall in the price of X (given the same money income) increases real income. Thus, a portion of the increase in the consumption of X is due to the fact that this individual has more real income. But there is a second reason as well. It is also the case that the fall in the price

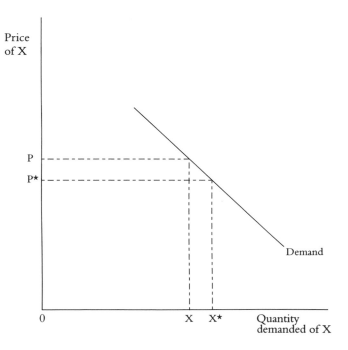

Figure 2.7   Two price–quantity combinations. If an individual is assumed to be a utility maximizer, a change in the price of any good will lead her to change her consumption of that good in the opposite direction. Thus, if the price of good X fell from P to P*, this individual would increase her consumption of this good from X to X*.

of X makes X cheaper relative to its substitutes. This fall in the relative price of X also leads this individual to increase the consumption of X. If you first examine these two effects separately, you can later determine what portion of the total change in the consumption of good X is due to an increase in real income and what portion is due to the decline in the relative price of X.

The Pure Income Effect   Figure 2.8 illustrates a pure income effect. This figure illustrates how an individual would change her consumption of X if her real income increased, holding the price of X constant. Because relative prices are illustrated by the slope of the income constraint, you hold relative prices constant by holding constant the slope of the income constraint. Shifting the income constraint to the right, parallel to itself, illustrates an

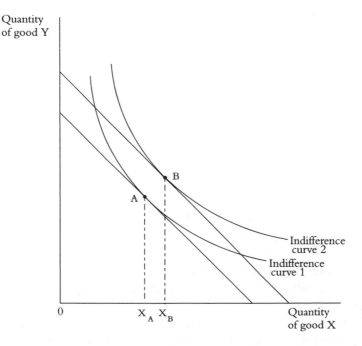

Figure 2.8   A pure income effect. A parallel shift to the right in the real income constraint illustrates an increase in real income, holding relative prices constant. (Relative prices are held constant because slopes of parallel lines are identical.) Whereas combination A had originally been the attainable combination that yielded the highest amount of total utility, combination B is now that combination. Combination B contains X_B of good X. Thus, an increase in real income increases the consumption of a good (if the good is a normal good).

increase in real income but holds relative prices constant. This illustrates that the relation between increases in real income and increases in the consumption of any good X is direct. Increases in real income lead this individual to increase her consumption of this good from X_A to X_B.

The direct relation between increases in real income and increases in the consumption of a good must be qualified. This direct relation holds for *normal* goods. Economists do not know in advance whether an increase in real income will increase or decrease the consumption of any particular good. But there are statistical findings that show that increases in real income (holding relative prices constant) sometimes do result in consumers reducing their purchases of particular goods. Potatoes and cheaper cuts of meat are two such goods. If an increase in real income (holding relative prices constant) leads an individual to reduce the consumption of a good, then the good is not a normal good but an *inferior* good.

The Pure Relative Price Effect   A fall in the price of X not only increases an individual's real income but also makes X cheaper relative to good Y. The individual thus has an incentive to increase the consumption of X for this reason as well. Figure 2.9 illustrates a pure relative price effect. This figure shows a change in relative prices, holding real income constant. Because real income constrains consumption and total utility depends on consumption, one holds real income constant by keeping this individual's total utility constant. Thus, keeping her on the same indifference curve illustrates constant real income. How does she respond to successive rises in the price of X, keeping her total utility constant? She buys successively less and less of good X as its price rises. This is illustrated in the figure by reductions in consumption from X_A to X_B to X_C.

Income and Relative Price Effects of a Fall in the Price of X   When the price of X falls, both the income effect and the relative price effect are triggered. Figures 2.6 and 2.7 illustrated the total change in the consumption of X that resulted from the fall in the price of X. Now you can disentangle that portion of the total change due to a rise in real income from that portion due to a fall in the relative price of X.

In Figure 2.10, the individual's initial best combination is U. This combination contains X_U of good X. The fall in the price of X enables her to attain a higher level of total utility represented by combination V. This combination contains X_V of good X. Thus, the fall in the price of X has led her to increase the consumption of X by the amount $X_U X_V$. This is the total effect. (This portion of Figure 2.10 merely replicates Figure 2.6.)

Consider first the relative price effect of the fall in the price of X. Change the slope of the initial income constraint so that it reflects the new price ratio, while keeping real income constant (that is, keeping her on indifference curve 2). When you do so, her best combination changes from U to W. Combination W contains more of good X (X_W rather than X_U). Thus, the relative price effect of the fall in the price of X increases the consumption of good X by the amount $X_U X_W$.

Illustrate the income effect of the price change by shifting the income constraint to the right, parallel to itself. This results in the best combination changing from W to V. Combination V contains X_V of good X. Thus, the income effect of the fall in the price of X reinforces the relative price effect, for the income effect leads this individual to increase further her consumption of X by the amount $X_W X_V$. Because the income effect has led to an increase in the consumption of this good, this good is a normal good.

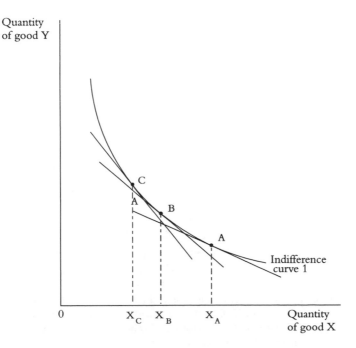

Figure 2.9   A pure relative price effect. Two changes in relative prices are illustrated by two changes in the slope of the real income constraint. However, because combinations A, B, and C are on the same indifference curve, real income is held constant. If the price of good X rises relative to good Y (holding real income constant), the individual decreases her consumption of that good from X_A to X_B to X_C.

2.7   THE MARKET DEMAND FOR X

This individual is not the only demander of good X. Other individuals also view X as a good. But individuals will differ from each other in the quantities of good X they will demand at various alternative prices of X. The market demand for X is a horizontal summation of the quantities demanded of X at various alternative prices of X by all individuals in the market for X. Figure 2.11 illustrates a market demand for X.

For simplicity, this market has three consumers. At price P the first individual buys 10 units, the second individual buys 20 units, and the third individual buys 3 units. The market quantity demanded at price P is 33. If

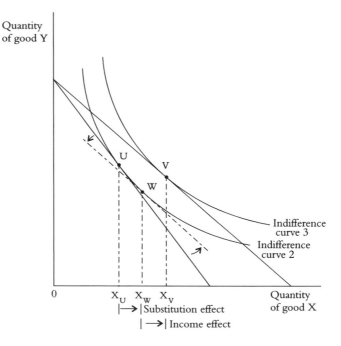

Figure 2.10   Disentangling the income and relative price effects of a decrease in the price of X. Given the individual's preferences, real income, and relative prices, combination U is her initial best combination. Combination U contains X_U of good X. The decrease in the price of X results in combination V now being the best combination. Combination V contains X_V of good X. Thus, $X_U X_V$ is total increase in the quantity demanded of X due to the fall in the price of X. $X_U X_W$ is the increase in the consumption of X due solely to the fact that the price of X has decreased relative to Y. $X_W X_V$ is the increase in the consumption of X due to an increase in real income.

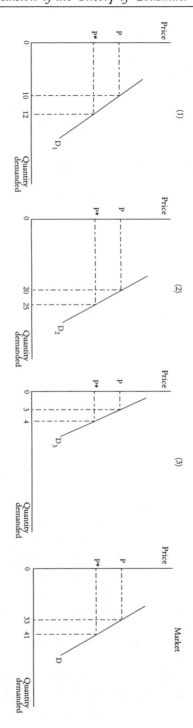

Figure 2.11 A market demand for X. If the price of X were P, then the market quantity demanded of X would be 33. If the price of X were P*, then the market quantity demanded of X would be 41. A market demand for X sums horizontally the quantities demanded of X by all market participants at various alternative prices of X.

the price of X falls to P*, all individuals increase their purchases of X, individual one from 10 to 12, individual two from 20 to 25, and individual three from 3 to 4. Thus, the market quantity demanded of X increases to 41. The market demand for any good X, then, is the summation of the quantities demanded of X at various alternative prices by all market participants. You will encounter the market demand for X again in Chapter 4.

2.8 ELASTICITY OF DEMAND FOR X

It is possible to estimate an elasticity coefficient for any relation between an independent and a dependent variable. Elasticity is the percentage change in the dependent variable divided by the percentage change in the independent variable. Consider, for example, the relation between highway accidents and highway speed. Without constructing a formal theory of highway accidents, you can take as given that the logical relation between the number of highway accidents (the dependent variable) and highway speed (one of a number of independent variables) is direct: other things equal, the faster highway speed, the greater will be the number of highway accidents. What if a 1 percent increase in average highway speed led (other things equal) to an increase of 2 percent in the number of highway accidents? The elasticity coefficient would be 2. Thus, elasticity measures the percentage change in the dependent variable in response to some percentage change in an independent variable. (This issue of elasticity was important in recent discussions in the United States about raising legal speed limits on interstate highways. Opponents of the increase argued that the probable increase in the number of highway deaths resulting from this change would be too high.)

Elasticity of Demand   The theory of consumer choice concludes that a decrease in the price of X will lead a utility-maximizing individual to change her consumption of X in the opposite direction. Now let's raise an additional question: how much will the consumption of X increase (measured as a percentage) if the price of X decreases (by some percentage amount)?

If the price of X were to decrease by 1 percent, how much would the quantity demanded of X increase? There are only three possibilities: by more than 1 percent, by 1 percent, or by less than 1 percent. Economists have names for these three possible outcomes. If a 1 percent decrease in the price of X leads to an increase in the quantity demanded of X of more than 1 percent, then demand is elastic. (Note carefully the terminology here. Economists do not say that X is elastic. It is the demand for X that is elastic.) If a 1 percent decrease in the price of X leads to an increase in the quantity demanded of

X of exactly 1 percent, then demand is unitarily elastic. If a 1 percent decrease in the price of X leads to an increase in the quantity demanded of X of less than 1 percent, then demand is inelastic. There are also two limit cases that have special names in economics. First, how elastic can demand be? How large an increase is possible in the quantity demanded of X if the price of X falls by 1 percent? The answer is: infinitely large. In this case, demand is perfectly elastic. Second, how inelastic can demand be? How small an increase in the quantity demanded of X is possible if the price of X falls by 1 percent? The answer is: zero. In this case, demand is perfectly inelastic. What factors influence how much the consumption of X will change in response to a change in its price?

Number and Closeness of Substitutes for X If X and Y are substitutes in consumption, then X and Y are both goods to an individual, and she is willing to substitute one of those goods for another at some (unspecified) rate. X and Y may not be good substitutes in any conventional sense, but they are substitutes nonetheless. Thus, economists might think of some individuals viewing children and houses as substitute goods and choosing to give up (at least for the time being) children in order to buy a house. On the other hand, if economists say that X and Y are good substitutes, they mean exactly what the public means. By contrast, the public tends to read too much into the word "substitute" and tends to think that if X and Y are substitutes, then they are perfect substitutes. To economists, perfect substitutes are not an interesting case; if X and Y are perfect substitutes, then X is Y. Individuals do make choices among substitutes; they do not make choices among perfect substitutes.

What do the number and closeness of substitutes have to do with elasticity of demand? A fall in the price of lemons not only decreases the absolute price of lemons but also decreases the price of lemons relative to that of limes and other substitutes. Individuals who currently consume limes and other substitutes for lemons now have an incentive to increase their consumption of lemons because of the fall in their price. The increase in the consumption of lemons will be greater, the larger the number of other goods that individuals view as substitutes for lemons and the closer those goods are viewed as substitutes. To generalize, the larger the number of substitutes for X and the closer those goods are as substitutes for X, the more elastic the demand for X.

The Percentage of Income Spent on X Consider a second determinant of the elasticity of demand for X: the percentage of an individual's income spent on X. Any rise in the price of X impacts adversely on an individual's

income and leads that individual to reduce her consumption of X. The greater
the percentage of income spent on X, the greater the adverse impact on her
budget, and the greater the reduction in her consumption of X given any
rise in its price. Thus, the greater the percentage of income spent on X, the
more elastic the demand for X.

Time for Adjustment When the price of X rises in a market, the consumption of X decreases immediately by some amount. As more time is
allowed for news of the price increase to spread and for consumers of X to
search out substitutes for X, the larger the decline in the consumption of X.
Thus, the longer the time allowed for adjustment, the more elastic will be
the demand for X.

2.9   CONTINUING THE ARGUMENT

Part I presents an overarching argument in the product market: the prices
that you pay for the various goods and services you consume will tend over
time toward the minimum per-unit total costs of producing them in purely
competitive product markets. The arguments in this chapter, while important
and challenging in themselves, nonetheless represent only one part of that
larger argument. Another necessary part of that larger argument is product
supply, the subject of Chapter 3.

2.10   QUESTIONS

1. The dependent variable in theories of economic growth is typically
   per-capita real income. What are the benefits to rising per-capita
   income in a nation?

2. Are crimes such as arson and rape goods to some individuals? If they
   are, what type of public policy would result in fewer of these crimes?

3. A firm's total revenue is the product of the price (P) of its output
   multiplied by its sales (Q) at that price: TR = (P)(Q). Because P
   and Q are inversely related, will an increase in product price increase
   total revenue or not?

4. Most individuals spend a tiny fraction of their income on salt.
   Furthermore, there are a small number of poor substitutes for salt.
   Thus, the demand for this good is highly inelastic. Nonetheless, a
   rise in the price of salt will reduce the consumption of salt. Where
   do you imagine this decline in consumption will come from?

3

Product Supply: A Conclusion of the Theory of Producer Choice

In this chapter, we construct the theory of producer choice (or the theory of the firm). Beginning again on the hypothesis of the self-interest-seeking individual, we will proceed step-by-step to a logical conclusion: product supply. Again, it is important to have a clear conception of our destination before setting out on this journey.

3.1 PRODUCT SUPPLY DEFINED

The supply of any good X is a relation between two variables: the price of X and the quantity supplied of X. In this relation, the quantity supplied of X is the dependent variable; the independent variable is the price of X. Figure 3.1 illustrates product supply.

The supply of X is subject to two equally valid interpretations. First, supply is a series of "if, then" statements. Thus, *if* the price of X were P, *then* this producer would supply the quantity Q. *If*, on the other hand, the price of X were P*, *then* this producer would supply a larger quantity Q*. Thus, the relation between these two variables is direct.

Alternatively, supply shows the minimum price at which producers of X are willing to supply various quantities of X. Thus, the minimum price at which this producer will be willing to supply the quantity Q is the price P. To induce this firm to increase its output to Q*, a higher minimum price P* is necessary.

The theory of producer choice begins with the same hypothesis that we used in the previous chapter: the self-interest-seeking individual. In Chapter 2, we employed a particular version of that general hypothesis: the individual

27

makes choices so as to maximize his own total utility. Here we employ a
different version of that same hypothesis: the producer is making choices so as to
maximize his total profits. (In both variants of this hypothesis, the individual
is pursuing his own interests through his actions, not the interest of others.)
This argument that we will construct in this chapter can be stated formally:
if a producer of X is assumed to maximize profits, then a change in the price
of X will lead him to change the quantity supplied of X in the same direction.

Economic profits are total revenues in excess of total costs. (Do not think
of profits as the difference between these two variables because that difference
can be a loss.) Firms generate revenues from the sale of output in product
markets. By contrast, firms incur costs by hiring inputs such as labor and
capital in a different set of markets: markets for factors of production. Thus,
in order to maximize profits a firm must keep its attention focussed simultaneously on these two sets of markets. As you begin to analyze the behavior of the
firm, however, you cannot examine both markets simultaneously. Thus, you
will set aside one set of these markets temporarily while examining the other.
Although you can examine either set of markets first, economists typically

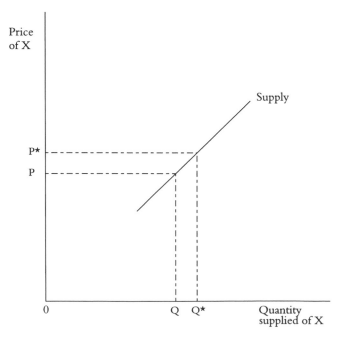

Figure 3.1   The supply of good X. The supply of X is a direct relation between
the price of X (the independent variable) and the quantity supplied of
X (the dependent variable).

begin the analysis of product supply by analyzing the market for factors of production.

3.2 SHORT-RUN PRODUCTION RELATIONS

In its simplest conception, production is the transformation of inputs into outputs. Input–output relations are engineering relations that economists do not normally study. However, these engineering relations are important to economists because they have implications for how the firm's costs of production vary with its output. Any firm assumed to maximize profits has to be concerned about how its costs vary with output.

Production   Any given quantity of output X can be produced using a variety of combinations of inputs. Figure 3.2 illustrates various combinations of two inputs, labor and capital, that can be used to produce various quantities of output. For example, 100 brooms can be produced using three units of capital and three units of labor, five units of capital and two units of labor, or any other combinations of these two inputs that lie on the isoquant ("equal quantity") labelled 100. Thus, that isoquant contains all combinations of two inputs that can be employed to produce an *equal quantity* of output – 100 brooms. The slope of an isoquant is dY/dX and is the rate at which a producer can make substitutions in production, keeping total output unchanged. If this rate were constant, the isoquant would be a straight line and would illustrate that capital and labor are perfect substitutes for each other. The fact that the isoquants in Figure 3.2 are convex with respect to the origin illustrates that capital and labor are substitutes in production, but not perfect substitutes.

Short-Run Production   Given enough time, a producer can increase his output by using more of either input (and no less of the other) or by using more of both inputs. For example, the producer in Figure 3.2 can increase the number of brooms from 100 to 190 by continuing to employ three units of capital but increasing the employment of labor from three to four, by continuing to employ three units of labor but increasing the employment of capital from three to six, or by using more of both inputs. However, this producer's options can be constrained by placing him in a set of circumstances defined as the *short run*.

The short run in the theory of the firm is that period of time during which at least one input in production cannot be changed. Do not think of the short run in terms of chronological time (like next July). Rather, think of the short run as a set of constraints placed on producers. If the producer in Figure 3.2

is in the short run, then at least one of his inputs cannot be changed. Assume for this discussion that the fixed input is capital, and that the quantity of capital is fixed at three units ($K^* = 3$). Then raise this question: how does this producer's output change as he changes the employment of labor, given that the capital used in production is fixed at three units?

If this producer increases incrementally his employment of labor from 2 to 10 workers (holding capital constant at three units), the data in Table 3.1 show that the producer's output rises from 50 brooms to 456 brooms. This same table shows, however, that these additional inputs of labor do not make equal contributions to the firm's total output. By hiring the third worker, the firm's output of brooms increases from 50 to 100. This increase in output of 50 brooms resulting from hiring one additional worker is the marginal physical product (MPP) of labor. The MPP of the fourth worker rises to 90 brooms. This phenomenon of an additional worker adding not only positive but also

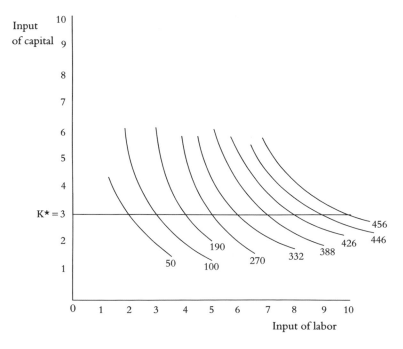

Figure 3.2   Production relations. Any given quantity of output can be produced using various combinations of inputs. The isoquants here illustrate those various combinations of capital and labor that can be employed to produce *equal quantities* of brooms. If the input of capital were to be fixed at three units, then increases in the output of brooms could be accomplished only by increasing the input that is not fixed: labor.

Table 3.1

Input of labor	Total product	Marginal physical product	Average physical product
2	50	...	25
3	100	50	33
4	190	90	47
5	270	80	54
6	332	62	55
7	388	56	56
8	426	38	54
9	446	20	50
10	456	10	46

Input-output relations in the short run. Holding capital fixed at 3 units, additional inputs of labor increase total product. But marginal physical product increases, then decreases, illustrating increasing, then decreasing, returns to labor.

increasing additions to output is increasing returns in production. Beginning with the fifth worker, however, the MPP of labor begins to decline. These additional workers do contribute positive additions to output. (Note carefully that total output rises by hiring the fifth and additional workers.) However, these workers contribute diminishing positive additions to output. This phenomenon of additional workers adding positive but diminishing additions to output is diminishing returns in production. Any particular production process may or may not be characterized by increasing returns in production in the short run. Diminishing returns, however, are characteristic of every production process in the short run.

Table 3.1 also presents the average physical product (APP) of labor. The APP of labor is the total product of labor divided by the number of workers employed. Thus, the average physical product of four workers is computed by dividing by four the total product produced by four workers.

The data in Table 3.1 are presented graphically in Figure 3.3. Notice that as long as the MPP of labor exceeds the APP in Figure 3.3 (b), the APP will rise. Thus, the MPP schedule intersects the APP schedule at the maximum APP.

There is nothing controversial about short-run production relations. If a producer increases the employment of a variable input while other inputs remain fixed, then diminishing returns to the variable input will eventually characterize production. This phenomenon in turn has important implications for the firm's costs of production in the short run.

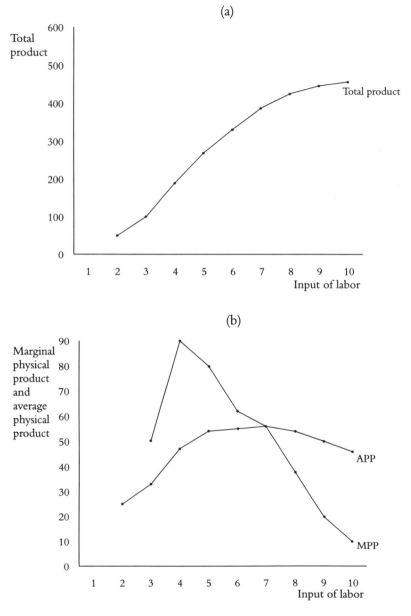

Figure 3.3 Total product, marginal product, and average product in the short run.
The data from Table 3.1 are graphed here. In the short run, increases
in the input of labor increase the total product (output) of brooms as
illustrated in panel (a). Panel (b) illustrates diminishing marginal returns
in production, as well as the relationship of marginal physical product
to average physical product.

3.3 SHORT-RUN COST RELATIONS

In short-run production relations, increases in inputs lead to increases in output. But because inputs are not available to the firm at no cost, increases in output increase costs. Short-run cost relations, then, connect two variables: output and costs of production in the short run.

Figure 3.4 (a) reproduces the general argument of diminishing returns in production we saw in Figure 3.3 (b). Figure 3.4 (b) traces out the marginal cost curve and the short-run average variable cost curve implied by these production relations.

Marginal Cost Marginal cost (MC) is the change in total costs (dTC) that results from changing output (dQ): MC = dTC/dQ. In the short run, the firm's employment of capital is fixed. Thus, a producer of brooms can increase the output of brooms in only one way in the short run: by increasing the employment of labor. Assume that the cost of capital (or some other fixed

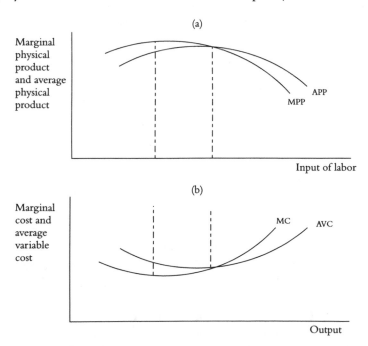

Figure 3.4   Diminishing returns and short-run costs. Because of diminishing returns in production, the firm's marginal costs of production in the short run will eventually rise. Because the MPP curve intersects the APP curve at the latter's maximum, the MC curve will intersect the AVC curve at the latter's minimum.

input) is $300 per unit time. As the firm hires additional inputs of labor at, say, $20 per unit time, its total costs change from $320 to $340, and so forth incrementally as it increases the employment of labor. But what of the denominator in MC? How is the output of brooms changing as the firm increases its employment of labor? Figure 3.4 (a) illustrates that increases in the input of labor produce varying effects on output. Initially, increasing the employment of labor yields increasing returns in production. Because the firm is hiring labor at a constant wage, increasing returns in production is the same phenomenon as decreasing MC. Thus, the MC of producing brooms declines as long as MPP rises.

However, increasing the employment of labor will at some point yield positive – but diminishing – returns to output in the short run. When diminishing returns begins to characterize the production process, the MC of producing brooms begins to rise.

Average Variable Cost   Average variable cost (AVC) is total variable cost (TVC) divided by output (Q): AVC = TVC/Q. Recall that APP rises as long as MPP is greater than APP. Thus, if MC is declining, then AVC will also decline as long as MC is less than AVC. Furthermore, just as the MPP schedule intersects the APP at the maximum value of the latter, the MC also intersects AVC at the AVC minimum.

Average Fixed Cost   Average fixed cost (AFC) is total fixed cost (TFC) divided by output (Q): AFC = TFC/Q. Total fixed costs do not vary with output. Thus, if the cost of capital is $300 per unit time, then this cost of producing brooms does not vary with output in the short run. AFC, however, steadily declines as more brooms are produced.

Average Total Cost   Average total cost (ATC) is total cost (TC) divided by output (Q): ATC = TC/Q. Because the TC of producing any output in the short run is the sum of TFC and TVC, the average total cost of producing any quantity of brooms is the sum of the AFC and AVC associated with that quantity.

A Family of Cost Relations in the Short Run   Figure 3.5 illustrates the four short-run cost relations. The MC curve declines and then rises, reflecting first increasing, then diminishing returns in production. The AVC curve declines as long as the MC lies below it, but rises when MC rises above it. The AFC curve declines throughout its entire length. The ATC for any level of output Q is simply the sum of the AFC and AVC for that level of output.

It is easy to get bogged down in the details of short-run cost relations. The overwhelmingly important point to realize, however, is quite simple: because diminishing returns in production are characteristic of every production process in the short run, the short-run costs of producing any output X will eventually rise. As you will see shortly, this reality will lead to a positively sloped supply curve of output in the short run.

3.4   MARGINAL REVENUE IN PURELY COMPETITIVE PRODUCT MARKETS

The producer who is assumed to maximize profits will choose to produce (and offer for sale) an additional unit of output if by doing so he adds more to his total revenues than to his total costs. The producer now has one piece of information that he needs in order to choose his level of output: he now knows how his total costs will change as he produces additional units of output. He now needs to know his marginal revenue (MR), how his total revenue will change (dTR) as he sells additional output (dQ): MR = dTR/dQ.

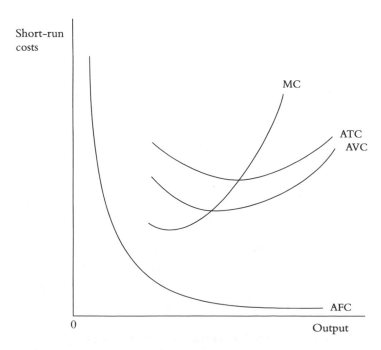

Figure 3.5   The firm's costs of production in the short run. As the firm increases output, average fixed costs steadily decline. Although the remainder of the firm's short-run cost functions also initially decline, they all eventually rise because of diminishing returns in production.

The Purely Competitive Model in the Product Market   Any model is a
construction. The model of pure competition contains two assumptions.
First, there are enough producers of X so that the actions of any one
producer (to produce more output or to go out of business, for example)
do not affect the price of X. Second, all producers of X are producing a
homogeneous product, a product that to consumers of X is alike in all
respects to the output of competing producers.

Although these two assumptions are typically presented from the point of
view of producers, consider these assumptions from the point of view of the
consumer of X. From the consumer's point of view, the first assumption
presents the consumer of X with the widest possible array of options in
consumption: all those producers who produce X. The second assumption
assures that consumers of X have no reason to prefer the output of one
producer over that of any other producer. To consumers, all producers of X
produce a product that is identical to the output of all other producers of X.

These two assumptions not only present the consumer of X with the
widest possible array of options in consumption. They also place a set of
constraints on producers of X. No producer of X can raise the price of X in
purely competitive product markets. Why not? Because consumers of X will
not pay a higher price for a product that they regard as identical in all respects
to the output of other producers of X. Thus, any producer of X who attempts to raise the price of X in purely competitive product markets will
discover that his sales not merely fall, but fall to zero.

Recall from the discussion of elasticity of demand in Chapter 2 that the
demand for X is elastic if some given percentage change in the price of X
causes the quantity demanded of X to change by a greater percentage. In
purely competitive product markets, consumer demand for any producer's
output is not merely elastic; it is perfectly elastic. Furthermore, this conclusion
accords with the earlier discussion of the determinants of the elasticity of
demand for X. We noted earlier that the larger the number of substitutes for
X and the closer those alternative goods are viewed as substitutes for X,
the more elastic will be the demand for X. In the model of pure competition,
the demand for X will be perfectly elastic because that model intentionally
confronts consumers of X with the widest possible array of perfect
substitutes in consumption.

In general, any producer of X who is assumed to maximize profits confronts
two alternative strategies for pursuing those profits. First, he can take actions
that raise total revenues. Second, he can act to lower costs. However, if a
producer is selling output in purely competitive product markets, the first
strategy ceases to be an option, for if a price increase causes sales to fall to zero,

his total revenues also fall to zero. No producer assumed to maximize profits would ever knowingly increase product-selling price if to do so would cause his total revenues to fall. In purely competitive product markets, however, total revenues do not merely fall, they fall to zero. Even though a perfectly elastic demand is theoretical overkill, it nonetheless effectively guarantees that profit-maximizing producers confront only one possible strategy to increase their profits in purely competitive markets: lowering their costs. As we will eventually see in some detail, the profit-maximizing activities of producers that are channelled into lowering costs inadvertently benefit consumers of X.

The Marginal Revenue Schedule in Purely Competitive Product Markets   Figure 3.6 presents the marginal revenue schedule for the producer who is selling output in purely competitive product markets. If X is brooms, then the price of brooms, P, is determined outside the firm by a set of forces

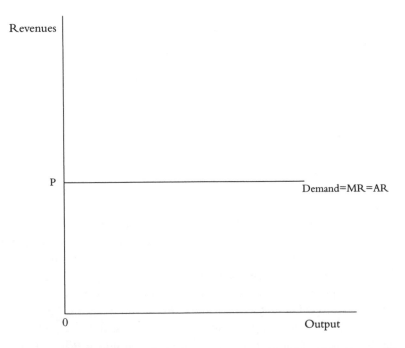

Figure 3.6   Revenue functions for the purely competitive firm. If the firm is selling its output in purely competitive product markets, the demand for its product is perfectly elastic at market price P. Because the firm can sell all of its output at the market-determined price, that price is also the firm's marginal revenue and its average revenue.

beyond the control of the firm. (In the following chapter, the precise set of forces that determine the price of any good X is presented and discussed.) At price P, this producer can sell all the brooms he chooses to sell. If the price of brooms is $2.00, and if the producer can sell all the brooms that he wishes to sell at that price, how does his total revenue change from selling additional brooms? By $2.00 per broom, the price of brooms. Thus, marginal revenue is the price of brooms: MR = P. Furthermore, marginal revenue ($2.00) is also average revenue (AR), defined as total revenue (TR) divided by sales of output (Q).

In Section 3.3, you discovered how the firm's total costs change as it produces additional units of output in the short run. Now you know how the firm's total revenues change as it sells additional units of output in purely competitive product markets. Thus, you now have enough information to conclude how much output this profit-maximizing producer will produce and offer for sale if the price of brooms were P.

3.5   ONE PRICE, ONE QUANTITY

Figure 3.7 illustrates information about the firm's costs as well as its revenues. Cost and revenues are on the vertical axis. Quantity of output is on the horizontal axis. For reasons that should now be well known, both the firm's costs and revenues vary with the output it produces and sells.

A firm that is assumed to maximize profits will follow a rule: it will produce and sell all units of output that add more to total revenues than to total costs (that is, all units of output for which MR > MC); it will not produce or sell any units of output that add more to total costs than to total revenues (that is, all units of output for which MC > MR). Following this rule, the firm illustrated in Figure 3.7 produces all units of output up to Q, because doing so will add more to its total revenues than to its total costs (that is, increase its profits). This firm does not produce any units of output beyond Q, because doing so will add more to its total costs than to its total revenues (that is, reduce its profits). Thus, the quantity of output that this profit-maximizing producer will produce and sell, given its cost and revenue functions, is Q. For this quantity, the addition to total revenue from selling this quantity (MR) is equal to the addition to total costs from producing it (MC). Thus, any profit-maximizing producer, now as always, will produce that quantity of output for which MR = MC.

Notice that this producer who chooses to produce and sell Q chooses to do so even though he is not making a profit. We know that this producer is not making a profit because the price (average revenue) from selling the

output Q is less than the average total costs (ATC) of producing it. Nonetheless, the producer chooses to produce and sell Q even though this
production is not profitable. Why is that? Why will a producer who is
assumed to maximize profits produce and sell output even though it is not
profitable to do so?

Note first that if this firm produces any output at all, given his cost and
revenue schedules, he will produce Q for the reasons already explained. The
relevant question, then, is why he chooses to produce Q at a loss rather than
zero output – producing zero output is always an option for a firm. The reason
is not complicated. By producing Q at price P, the firm generates revenues
sufficient to pay all of its variable costs. (AR for output Q exceeds the AVC
of producing it.) Furthermore, there are revenues sufficient to pay some (but
not all) of its fixed costs. If the firm ceases operations, it loses all of its fixed
costs. So, by continuing to produce and sell Q, the producer minimizes his
losses. This consideration requires a minor adjustment in the previous
conclusion: a producer will produce and sell that quantity of output for which

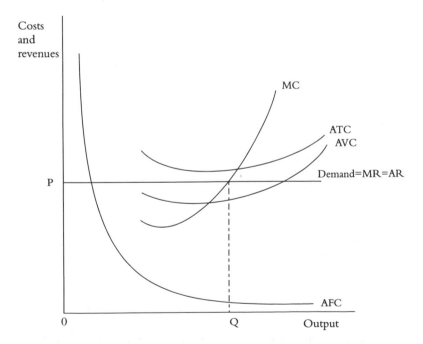

Figure 3.7   One price, one quantity. If the firm is assumed to be a profit-maximizing producer, then it will choose to produce Q, the quantity of
output for which the addition to total cost from producing it (MC) is
equal to the addition to total revenue from selling it (MR).

MR = MC as long as marginal revenue (MR) exceeds the average variable cost (AVC) for that level of output.

Is the quantity Q at price P supply? No, it is not. Supply is a series of "if, then" statements. Thus, it is necessary to confront this producer with a higher price of X and see why he chooses to increase the quantity supplied at this higher price.

3.6 REACHING THE CONCLUSION

Figure 3.8 illustrates a rise in the price of X from P to P*. As a result of the rise in the price of X (for reasons that you can ignore at present), the demand for this firm's output becomes perfectly elastic at the higher price P*. Thus, P* is also MR* and AR*. How does this producer adjust to the rise in the price of X?

The hatched area of Figure 3.8 illustrates the potential addition to profits that results from the rise of the price of X. This producer can capture those

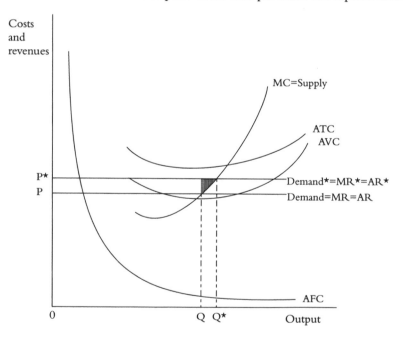

Figure 3.8   The consequence of a rise in the price of X. If the price of X rises from P to P*, then Q is no longer the level of output that maximizes profits. The firm can increase its profits (the hatched area) by increasing output to Q*. Thus, if the price of X rises, a profit-maximizing firm will increase the quantity supplied of X.

profits by expanding output from Q to Q*. For each unit of output produced from Q to Q*, marginal revenue (which has increased) exceeds marginal cost (which has not changed). Thus, every unit of output from Q to Q* increases this producer's profits.

Supply is a series of "if, then" statements. What schedule determines the quantity supplied of X at various alternative prices of X? It is the marginal cost curve that solves for quantity, given price. Thus, that portion of the marginal cost curve that lies above the AVC curve is the firm's supply curve of output in the short run in purely competitive markets. It now becomes clear why any producer of X will be willing to increase the quantity supplied of X in the short run, but only at higher prices of X. The reason is that additional output of X is produced in the short run at rising cost, and a profit-maximizing producer will require higher prices to compensate for those higher costs.

Like any other theoretical statement, product supply is a logical prediction of the expected direction of change in the dependent variable given any change in the independent variable. Having now reproduced the theory of producer choice and reached product supply as a conclusion, the overall argument can be summarized as follows: *if* a producer is assumed to maximize profits, *then* a change in the price of X will lead him to change in the same direction the quantity of X that he produces and supplies. Thus, product supply is a direct relation between these two variables.

3.7 MARKET SUPPLY

This producer is not the only producer of X. Assume for simplicity that there are two other producers of X in this market. Figure 3.9 illustrates market supply in a market with three suppliers. At a price of $2.00, firm one produces 10 units, firm two produces 20 units, and firm three produces 5 units. Thus, the market quantity supplied of X at price $2.00 is 35. As the price of X rises to $2.10, all producers of X increase their output. Firm one increases output from 10 to 12; firm two increases output from 20 to 23; firm three from 5 to 6. Thus, the total quantity supplied of X in this market at the higher price is 41. The market supply of X is the total quantity supplied of X by all firms in the market at various alternative prices of X. Like the individual supply curves, the market supply of X also has a positive slope.

3.8 ELASTICITY OF SUPPLY OF X

How much will the quantity supplied of X increase given a rise in the price of X? This is the question of elasticity of product supply. Because changes in

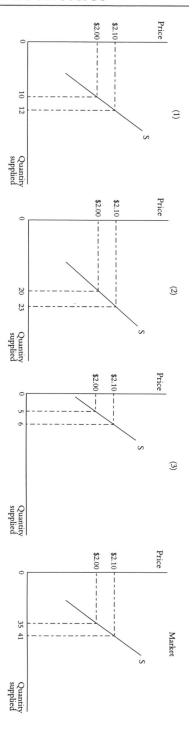

Figure 3.9   A market supply curve of X. If the price of X were $2.00, then the market quantity supplied at that price by all the firms in the market would be 35. If the price of X rises to $2.10, then the market quantity supplied increases to 41. The market supply curve of X illustrates the quantity supplied by all producers in the market at various alternative prices of X.

both price and quantity are measured as percentage changes, elasticity of product supply is the percentage change in the quantity supplied of X (the dependent variable) divided by the percentage change in the price of X (the independent variable).

Because the price of X is the independent variable, introduce some percentage change in the price of X. But because the computation of elasticity requires dividing that percentage change into the percentage change in the dependent variable, choose a percentage change easy to work with. If, for example, the price of X changes by 1 percent, how much will the quantity supplied of X change in response? Again, there are three possibilities: by more than 1 percent, by 1 percent, or by less than 1 percent. If a 1 percent change in the price of X leads the quantity supplied of X to change by more than 1 percent, then supply is elastic. If a 1 percent change in the price of X leads to a change in the quantity supplied of X of exactly 1 percent, then supply is unitarily elastic. If a 1 percent change in the price of X leads to a change in the quantity supplied of X of less than 1 percent, then supply is inelastic. There are again two limit cases. It is possible for supply to be perfectly elastic. This would be the case if a 1 percent change in the price of X led to an infinitely large change in the quantity supplied of X. Finally, supply may be perfectly inelastic. This would be the case if a 1 percent change in the price of X led to a zero change in the quantity supplied of X.

Availability of Inputs   A producer of X has an incentive to increase the output of X as its price rises. The question then arises: how readily available for employment are the additional resources needed to increase the output of X? For example, can some resources currently being used to produce Y be shifted into the increased production of X? Are there unemployed resources? The more easily additional inputs can be shifted into the production of X, the more elastic will be the supply of X.

Time for Adjustment   Time is a factor that makes both demand and supply more elastic. As noted earlier, all producers of X have an incentive to increase the output of X as its price rises. It may be possible for a producer to increase his output to some degree immediately. For example, a producer may be able to increase output by working existing employees longer hours. Given enough time, however, the producer can recruit and train additional workers. Thus, the longer the time allowed for producers of X to adjust to a rise in the price of X, the greater will be the increase in the quantity supplied of X.

3.9   CONTINUING THE ARGUMENT

You have now taken another large step in the overarching argument in Part I: in purely competitive product markets, the prices that consumers pay for the various goods and services they consume will tend, over time, toward the minimum per-unit total costs of producing them. The arguments in this chapter are a necessary part of that larger argument. But the factors that determine product price in purely competitive markets have not yet been identified. Thus, this argument continues into Chapter 4. Chapter 4 presents a model of equilibrium price determination and identifies those market forces that cause the price of X to change over time.

3.10   QUESTIONS

1. Assume that you are preparing for a test in this course. As you engage in this production process (the transformation of inputs into output), what inputs are fixed? Identify diminishing returns to the variable input in this production process.

2. Why is the demand for the output of the purely competitive firm perfectly elastic rather than merely elastic? (Recall the determinants of elasticity of product demand from Chapter 2.)

3. If a purely competitive firm is experiencing economic losses, it can always raise its product price to increase its total revenues. True or false, and explain.

———— 4 ————

A Model of Equilibrium Price Determination

In Chapter 2, we assumed various alternative prices of X and found that a utility-maximizing individual changes the consumption of X in the opposite direction from the change in the price of X. Similarly, in Chapter 3, we assumed various alternative prices of X and established that a profit-maximizing producer of X changes the quantity supplied of X in the same direction as the change in the price of X. In this chapter, we will examine those factors that determine the equilibrium price and quantity of X. In addition, the market forces that cause the equilibrium price and quantity of X to change will be identified and discussed.

4.1 EQUILIBRIUM PRICE AND QUANTITY OF X

Before we examine the model of equilibrium price determination, we must first consider the concept of equilibrium.

Equilibrium Equilibrium refers to the state in which there is "no net tendency to change." Thus, if an individual is at her equilibrium weight, her weight exhibits no net tendency to change. There are, of course, theories that set out to explain the determinants of equilibrium weight, but those theories are beside the point here. Regardless of the causes of equilibrium weight, an equilibrium weight is by definition a weight that exhibits no net tendency to change.

Similarly, an equilibrium price is a price that exhibits no net tendency to change. In Figure 4.1, P_E is an equilibrium price; it exhibits no net tendency to change. By contrast, if the price of X were P, that price would exhibit a net tendency to change to P_E. Why is P not an equilibrium price?

45

Surpluses In Figure 4.1, the market demand for X is labelled D, and the market supply of X is labelled S. If the price of X were P, then the market quantity demanded of X would be Q_D. At price P, however, the market quantity supplied of X would be larger – Q_S. The amount by which the market quantity supplied of X exceeds the market quantity demanded of X at price P is a surplus (or excess supply) of X. If a surplus exists at P, P is not an equilibrium price. Thus, P will exhibit a net tendency to change. In which direction will P change to approach its equilibrium value?

Given a surplus of X, there is a net tendency for the price of X to fall. As the price of X begins to fall, two adjustments take place that tend to narrow the surplus. First, at lower prices consumers of X increase the quantities they consume of X. Second, at lower prices producers of X decrease the quantity they produce and sell. As long as a surplus (excess

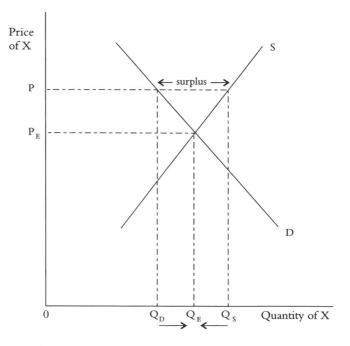

Figure 4.1   A surplus of X at price P. Given the market demand for X and the market supply of X, a surplus of X would exist at price P. The surplus of X decreases the price of X. As the price of X falls, consumers of X increase their purchases of X; suppliers of X decrease their production of X. The price of X continues to fall until it reaches its equilibrium value, P_E. At price P_E, the equilibrium quantity of X is Q_E.

supply) exists, price continues to fall so as to eliminate the surplus. At what price has the surplus been eliminated? At price P_E, there is no surplus. At that price, the market quantity demanded of X (Q_E) just equals the market quantity supplied of X (also Q_E). There exist, then, no further net tendencies for the price of X to fall. Thus, P_E is an equilibrium price and Q_E is an equilibrium quantity.

Shortages By contrast, consider Figure 4.2. Again, the market supply of X is labelled S, and D is the market demand for X. If the price of X were P, then the market quantity supplied of X would be Q_S. But the market quantity demanded of X would be greater – Q_D. The amount by which the market quantity demanded exceeds the market quantity supplied at price P is a shortage of (or excess demand for) X. If a shortage exists at price P, then P is not an equilibrium price. There will be a net tendency for that price to

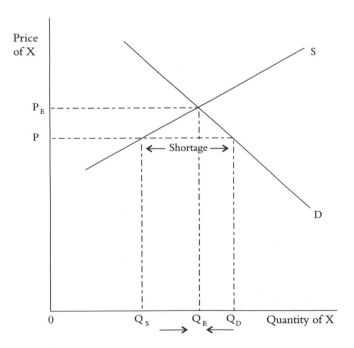

Figure 4.2   A shortage of X at price P. Given the market demand for X and the market supply of X, a shortage of X would exist at P. The shortage of X increases the price of X. As the price of X rises, consumers of X decrease their purchases of X; suppliers of X increase their production of X. The price of X continues to rise until it reaches its equilibrium value, P_E. At price P_E, the equilibrium quantity of X is Q_E.

change. In which direction will the price of X change so as to reach its equilibrium value?

Given a shortage, there is a net tendency for the price of a good to rise. As the price of X begins to rise toward its equilibrium value, two adjustments occur that eliminate the shortage. First, at higher prices producers increase output. Thus, the market quantity supplied of X increases. Second, at higher prices consumers of X tend to reduce the quantity of X they consume. Thus, the market quantity demanded of X tends to decrease. Price continues to rise until it reaches its equilibrium value P_E. At that price, the market quantity supplied of X (Q_E) equals the market quantity demanded of X (also Q_E). There exist, then, no further net tendencies for the price of X to rise. Thus, P_E is an equilibrium price and Q_E is an equilibrium quantity.

Two Immediate Implications of the Model   There are two implications that flow immediately from this simple model of product–price determination. First, because downward price adjustments eliminate surpluses in product markets, economists would be surprised to see chronic surpluses in product markets where prices are allowed to adjust downward. Similarly, because upward price adjustments eliminate shortages in product markets, economists would be surprised to see chronic shortages in product markets where price is allowed to adjust upward. The word "surprise" is used deliberately here. Something is surprising if it is unexpected. Economists would not only be surprised but also dumbfounded to discover either chronic surpluses or shortages in product markets where price is allowed to adjust to reach its equilibrium value.

But economists would not be surprised to see chronic surpluses in product markets where price is not allowed to adjust downward to reach its equilibrium value, nor would they be surprised to see chronic shortages in product markets where price is not allowed to adjust upward to reach its equilibrium value. Both the chronic surpluses and the chronic shortages would be expected.

If price P_E in both Figures 4.1 and 4.2 were an equilibrium price of X, what would cause the equilibrium price of X to change?

4.2   CHANGES IN THE MARKET DEMAND FOR X

Because the equilibrium price of X is determined by the interaction of the market demand for X and the market supply of X, any change in the market demand for X will lead, in turn, to a change in the equilibrium price of X. What does it mean to say that the market demand for X changes?

An Increase in the Market Demand for X   We learned in Chapter 2 that demand is subject to two equally valid interpretations. First, demand is a series of "if, then" statements. Second, demand illustrates the maximum price that an individual will pay for various quantities of X. Because demand is subject to two equally valid interpretations, increases in demand will also be subject to two equally valid interpretations.

Figure 4.3 illustrates an increase in the market demand for X from D to D*. Both of these demands are a series of "if, then" statements. Furthermore, both of these market demands show the maximum price that consumers of X will pay for various quantities of X. How then do they differ? In the first case, if the price of X were P, then the market quantity demanded of X would be Q. Now, given an increase in the market demand for X, the market quantity demanded at price P is larger – Q*. There is nothing unique about this particular price and quantity. At every price, the quantity demanded of X is

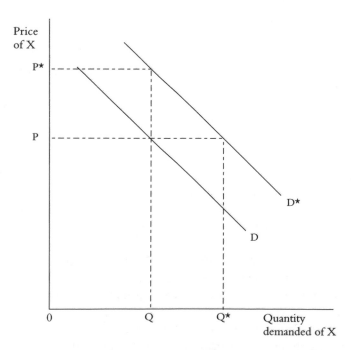

Figure 4.3   An increase in the market demand for X. The market demand for X increases from D to D*. Whereas the quantity demanded of X at price P had been Q in this market, the quantity demanded at that price is now greater: Q*. Similarly, whereas the maximum price that individuals in this market had been willing to pay for the quantity Q had been P, now that maximum price is higher: P*.

now greater than it was. Thus, an increase in the market demand for X increases the quantity demanded of X at every price.

Similarly, it is also correct to say that an increase in the market demand for X increases the maximum price that consumers of X are willing to pay for various quantities. Thus, the maximum price that demanders of X are willing to pay for the quantity Q is now P* rather than P. There is nothing unique about this particular price and quantity. The maximum price that consumers of X are willing to pay rises for every quantity. Thus, an increase in the market demand for X increases the maximum price that consumers of X are willing to pay for every quantity.

A Decrease in the Market Demand for X   Figure 4.4 illustrates a decrease in the market demand for X. Originally, if the price of X were P, the market quantity demanded of X was Q. Now, because of the decline in the market demand for X, the market quantity demanded at price P is less – Q*. Furthermore, the market quantity demanded of X at every price is less than it was. Thus, one interpretation of a decrease in the market demand for X is a decrease in the market quantity demanded of X at every price.

Similarly, the maximum price that consumers had been willing to pay for the quantity Q was P. Now that maximum price has fallen to P* for that quantity. Furthermore, the maximum price that consumers of X are willing to pay for each quantity is less than it was. Thus, it is also correct to say that a decrease in the market demand for X decreases the maximum price that consumers of X are willing to pay for every quantity.

There are numerous factors that lead to a change in the market demand for X. Any factor that causes the market demand for X to change will have a further effect: the equilibrium price and quantity of X will also change. What factors cause the market demand for X to increase?

A Rise in the Price of Substitutes for X   Lemons (good X) and limes (good Y) are substitutes in consumption. If the price of limes (Y) rises, will the demand for lemons (X) change? Walk through this argument a step at a time.

What is the first effect of a rise in the price of Y? The law of demand concludes that the quantity demanded of Y will decline. But there is a further effect. As individuals reduce their consumption of limes (Y) as its price rises, they search for substitutes. If X is a substitute for Y, then there will be an increase in the market quantity demanded of X at every price. But this is an increase in the market demand for X: an increase in the market quantity demanded of X at every price. Thus, a rise in the price of Y, where Y is a substitute for X in consumption, increases the market demand for X. Or, to state this argument in terms of limes and lemons, a rise in the price of limes increases the market demand for lemons.

Figure 4.5 illustrates that an increase in the market demand for X has further effects on the equilibrium price and quantity of X. Originally, the equilibrium price and quantity of X had been P and Q. However, as the market demand for X increases from D to D*, an excess demand for X is created at price P. The market quantity demanded of X (Q*) now exceeds the market quantity supplied of X (Q) at that price. Excess demand leads to an increase in both equilibrium price and quantity. Thus, the price of X begins to rise toward its new equilibrium value P_E. As price begins to rise two adjustments eliminate the shortage. First, producers expand output at higher prices. Second, consumers cut back on their purchases of X at higher prices. The upward price

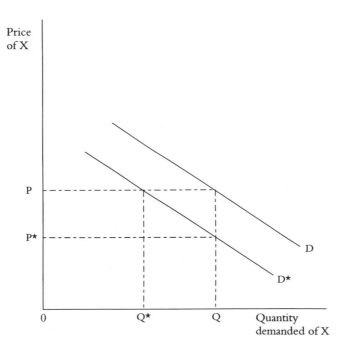

Figure 4.4   A decrease in the market demand for X. The market demand for X decreases from D to D*. Whereas the quantity demanded of X at price P had been Q in this market, the quantity demanded at that price is smaller: Q*. Similarly, whereas the maximum price that individuals in this market had been willing to pay for the quantity Q had been P, now that maximum price is lower: P*.

adjustment eliminates the shortage, and a new equilibrium is established at price P_E and quantity Q_E.

This discussion can be summarized in this manner: if X and Y are substitutes in consumption, then a rise in the price of Y increases the market demand for X, leading in turn to an increase in both the equilibrium price and quantity of X.

A Decrease in the Price of a Complement   If good Z is a complement of good X in consumption, then the two goods are used together in consumption. Thus, tea (Z) and lemon (X) are complements in consumption to many people. Is there any connection between a decrease in the price of Z and the demand for X?

What is the first effect of a decrease in the price of tea (Z)? The law of demand concludes that a decrease in the price of Z will lead consumers of Z

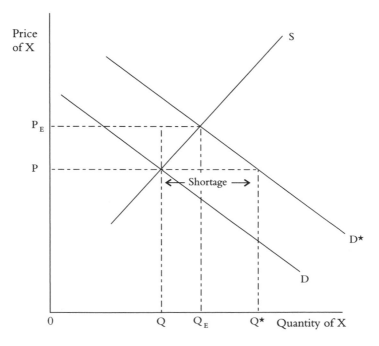

Figure 4.5   The effects of an increase in the market demand for X on the equilibrium price and quantity of X. The market demand for X increases from D to D*. The increase in the market demand for X creates a shortage of X at price P. The shortage of X is eliminated by a rise in the price of X to its new equilibrium value: P_E. At that price, the new equilibrium quantity of X becomes Q_E.

to increase their consumption of Z. But there is a further effect. Goods Z and X are used together. Because the consumption of Z has increased, the market quantity demanded of X will now be greater at every price. This is, of course, an increase in the market demand for X. Thus, if tea and lemons are complements in consumption, a decrease in the price of tea increases the market demand for lemons.

An increase in the market demand for X (lemons) has the same additional effects discussed earlier. The increase in the market demand for X creates excess demand for X at price P. A new equilibrium is restored at a higher equilibrium price P_E and quantity Q_E. This argument can be summarized as follows: where Z and X are complements in consumption, a decrease in the price of Z increases the market demand for X and increases both the equilibrium price and quantity of X.

An Increase in Income If X is a normal good, an increase in the income of consumers increases the market demand for X. As before, increases in the market demand for X lead in turn to an increase in both the equilibrium price and quantity of X.

An Increase in Population An increase in population in a market increases the market demand for X. This increase in the market demand for X also has further effects: both the equilibrium price and quantity of X increase.

Price Expectations If consumers of X expect the price of X to be higher in the future than at present, then they will increase their purchases at every price in the present. Thus, the market demand for X increases in the present, increasing both the equilibrium price and quantity of X.

Changes in Tastes and Preferences If, for some reason, consumers of X now receive more utility from consuming X than they used to, the market demand for X will increase, leading to increases in both the equilibrium price and quantity of X.

Determinants of Increases in the Market Demand for X: A Summary
The market demand for X will increase if:

1. the price of Y rises, and Y is a substitute for X in consumption.
2. the price of Z declines, and Z is a complement of X in consumption.
3. consumer income increases (given that X is a normal good).

4. population increases.

5. consumers expect that the price of X will be higher in the future than in the present.

6. there is a change in consumer tastes and preferences toward X.

Each of these arguments could be reversed to illustrate decreases in the market demand for X. Decreases in the market demand for X cause an excess supply of X, leading to declines in both equilibrium price and quantity of X. However, the phenomena of excess supply and decreasing equilibrium price and quantity will be illustrated by increases in the market supply of X.

4.3   CHANGES IN THE MARKET SUPPLY OF X

Because the equilibrium price and quantity of X are determined by the interaction of the market demand for X and the market supply of X, any factor that causes the market supply of X to change will affect the equilibrium price and quantity of X. What does it mean to say that the market supply of X changes?

Decreases in the Market Supply of X   Figure 4.6 illustrates a decrease in the market supply of X from S to S*. Both of these supply curves are series of "if, then" statements, and they both can be interpreted as showing the minimum prices that producers of X will be willing to supply various quantities of X. How then do the two supply curves differ?

Originally, the market quantity supplied of X at P was Q. Now, the market quantity supplied at P is less – Q*. Furthermore, there is nothing unique about price P. More generally, what has occurred is a decrease in the market quantity supplied at every price. Thus, one interpretation of a decrease in the market supply of X is: the market quantity of X that producers will supply at every price is now less than it was before.

But there is an alternative interpretation that is equally true. Whereas producers of X were willing to supply the quantity Q at price P, now they require a higher price (P*) to supply that same quantity. More generally, producers now require a higher price for each quantity that they produce and offer for sale. Thus, it is also true to say that if the market supply of X decreases, then the minimum price at which producers are willing to supply every quantity is now higher than it was before.

But the market supply of X can also increase. What does it mean to say that the market supply of X increases?

Increases in the Market Supply of X   Figure 4.7 illustrates an increase in the market supply of X from S to S*. Originally, the market quantity supplied of X at price P was Q. Now the market quantity supplied of X at that price is a larger amount – Q*. Furthermore, the market quantity supplied of X at every price is larger than it was before. Thus, if the market supply of X increases, then the quantity supplied of X at every price is greater than it was before.

Similarly, an increase in the market supply of X has a second equally valid interpretation. Whereas the minimum price at which producers of X were willing to supply the quantity Q used to be P, now that minimum price has declined to P*. Furthermore, the minimum price that producers of X are willing to supply all quantities is now less than it was. Thus, an increase in the market supply of X decreases the minimum price that producers of X are willing to supply every quantity.

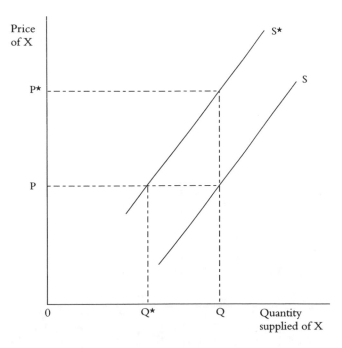

Figure 4.6   A decrease in the market supply of X. The market supply of X decreases from S to S*. Suppliers of X had been willing to supply the quantity Q at price P. Now the quantity of X supplied at that price has decreased to Q*. Similarly, whereas P had formerly been the minimum price at which suppliers of X had been willing to supply Q, that minimum price has now risen to P*.

What factors lead to increases in the market supply of X? What are the effects on the equilibrium price and quantity of X of increases in the market supply of X?

Decreases in the Price of an Input   Recall from Chapter 3 that a firm's supply curve is a cost curve. In particular, for the producer who sells output in purely competitive product markets, the supply curve in the short run is that portion of its marginal cost curve that lies above its average variable cost curve. Because the firm's supply curve is a cost curve, any change that lowers a firm's costs of production will increase its supply of output.

A firm's costs of production depend on two variables: (1) the prices of the inputs that it employs and (2) the productivity of those inputs. Given the productivity of an input, a decrease in the price of that input lowers the costs of producing X, thus increasing the supply of X.

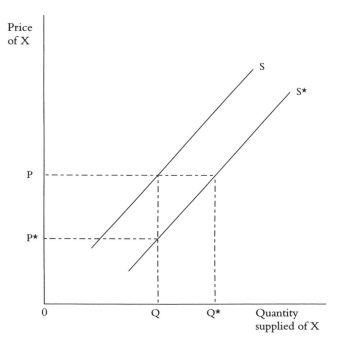

Figure 4.7   An increase in the market supply of X. The market supply of X increases from S to S*. Suppliers of X had been willing to supply the quantity Q at price P. Now the quantity of X supplied at that price has increased to Q*. Similarly, whereas P had formerly been the minimum price at which suppliers of X had been willing to supply Q, that minimum price has now fallen to P*.

Figure 4.8 illustrates the increase in the market supply of X and the effects of this change on the equilibrium price and quantity of X. The first effect of the increase in the market supply of X is the creation of an excess supply of X at price P. The market quantity supplied of X has increased to Q^* at that price, but the market quantity demanded of X remains Q. The emergence of excess supply in this market leads to a fall in the price of X. As price begins to fall toward its new equilibrium value, two sets of adjustments are triggered. First, as the price falls, consumers of X increase their purchases of X. Second, as price falls, producers of X cut back on current production. The final consequences of the increase in the market supply of X are a lower equilibrium price of $X(P_E)$ and a higher equilibrium quantity of $X(Q_E)$.

Summarizing this argument, a decrease in the price of an input used to produce X increases the market supply of X, thus decreasing the equilibrium price of X but increasing the equilibrium quantity of X.

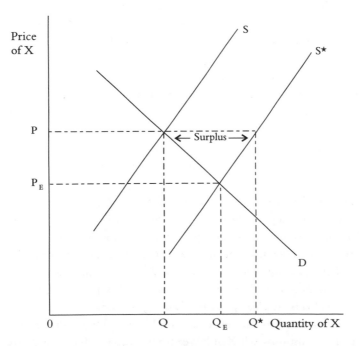

Figure 4.8   The effects of an increase in the market supply of X on the equilibrium price and quantity of X. The market supply of X increases from S to S^*, creating a surplus of X at price P. The surplus of X is eliminated by a fall in the price of X to its new equilibrium value: P_E. At that price, the new equilibrium quantity is Q_E.

An Improvement in the Productivity of an Input   Given the price of an input, an improvement in its productivity lowers the costs of producing output. As before, a reduction in the costs of producing X increases the market supply of X. Increases in the market supply of X decrease the equilibrium price of X and increase the equilibrium quantity of X.

Price Expectations   If producers expect that the price of X will be lower in the future than at present, they will increase the market supply of X in the present, thus decreasing the equilibrium price of X but increasing the equilibrium quantity of X.

A Decrease in the Price of an Alternative Output   Assume that producers of lemons (X) can also produce limes (Y). A decrease in the price of limes (Y) will increase the supply of lemons (X). The logic of this argument proceeds in two steps.

First, what is the initial effect on producers of a decrease in the price of limes (Y)? Producers of limes reduce the quantity supplied of limes. This adjustment is the law of supply with reference to limes.

However, producers who can produce both lemons and limes transfer some resources from the production of limes to the production of lemons. Because there are now more resources used in the production of lemons (X), there is a larger quantity supplied of lemons in the market at every price than there was before. In short, the market supply of lemons increases in Figure 4.8 from S to S^*. That increase, in turn, decreases the equilibrium price of lemons to P_E and increases the equilibrium quantity of lemons to Q_E.

Number of Producers   An increase in the number of producers of X increases the market supply of X, thus having the predictable effects: the equilibrium price of X falls; the equilibrium quantity of X increases.

Note that an increase in the number of producers of X has two effects that are beneficial to consumers. First, there is a larger equilibrium quantity of X produced and consumed. Second, consumers of X pay lower prices for X. These two effects are clearly to the advantage of consumers of X. Note also, however, that these consequences are not beneficial to producers of X. Producers of X must now sell X at lower prices, and producers of X are better off (given their costs) with higher (not lower) prices for the goods they produce and sell. It would clearly be to the advantage of producers of X to stop the entry of new producers into the market for X if they could. In purely competitive product markets, producers have no such power. In actual markets, however, many producers do have such power. We will pursue this point at greater length in subsequent chapters.

The Determinants of Changes in Market Supply: A Summary The market supply of X will increase if:

1. the price of an input used to produce X decreases.
2. there is an improvement in the productivity of inputs used to produce X.
3. producers of X expect that the price of X will be lower in the future than in the present.
4. the price of Y decreases, and Y is an alternative output that producers of X can produce.
5. there is an increase in the number of producers of X.

Increases in the market supply of X have, in turn, two further effects. First, the equilibrium price of X decreases. Second, the equilibrium quantity of X increases.

4.4 CONTINUING THE ARGUMENT

In this chapter, we have taken another substantial step toward reaching the conclusion first introduced in Chapter 2: the prices of the goods and services you consume will tend in the long run toward the minimum per-unit total costs of producing them in purely competitive product markets. You have now learned why the price of some good X is what it is and have identified those forces that change the price of X over time. In the face of the many influences on product price identified and discussed in this chapter, why would anyone expect the price of X in purely competitive product markets to tend over time toward the minimum per-unit total costs of producing it? The logic of this conclusion is presented in the following chapter in which we will take the final step to reaching the conclusion set forth in Part I.

4.5 QUESTIONS

1. A state like Florida that experiences very rapid population growth will have very rapidly rising housing prices. True or false, and explain.
2. Federal legislation prevents the prices of several farm commodities

from falling. (a) What happens to the surplus of farm commodities? (b) At the supported prices, farmers have an incentive to produce more output. How can they be prevented from producing more output at the higher supported prices?

3. How does a decrease in tariff barriers on foreign-produced cars erode the profits of American car producers?

4. It is virtually impossible to introduce productivity gains in the performing arts. (Orchestras cannot be made to play Mozart symphonies twice as fast.) In light of this, what will be the effect of rising wages of musicians on the equilibrium price and quantity of symphony tickets?

5. The market price of compact disc players has steadily decreased alongside steadily increasing sales. How are these price and output changes possible in the face of (a) rising incomes and population growth and (b) rising prices of inputs?

5

Long-Run Tendencies in Purely Competitive Product Markets

In the short run in purely competitive product markets, the price of X may be above, below, or equal to the average total costs (ATC) of producing X. There is no logical argument in economic theory that necessitates any particular one of these outcomes in the short run. However, in the long run, there is only one logical outcome: in purely competitive markets, product price will tend toward the minimum average total costs of producing the product. Note carefully the strength of this conclusion. Economic theory does not conclude merely that price tends toward the average total costs of producing the product; that conclusion can hold in the short run as firms earn zero profits. The conclusion that we will reach is that the price consumers pay for the various goods and services they consume will tend toward the minimum average total costs of producing that output in the long run, after firms have made all the possible adjustments they can make over time to lower their costs.

This conclusion can be stated a second way. To say that the price consumers pay for goods and services will tend in the long run to equal the minimum average total costs of producing them is identical to saying that producers' economic profits will tend toward zero in the long run in purely competitive product markets. Stated this way, this conclusion may alarm some individuals. If producers cannot make economic profits, how can they stay in business? This concern is defused once it is clearly grasped what economists mean by this conclusion.

5.1 ZERO ECONOMIC PROFITS

All factors of production have alternative uses. In the theory of producer choice, the firm's costs of production are those payments necessary to keep

61

all factors of production employed with the firm so they are not lost to alternative uses. In any clear discussion of economic profits, it is imperative to speak separately of two different categories of costs: explicit costs and implicit costs.

The explicit costs of production are all those direct payments, such as wages, that are necessary to keep factors of production from moving to their next best alternative employment. In other words, the wages a firm pays must be equal to the opportunity cost of labor if the firm expects to attract and retain labor.

Other inputs have alternative uses but may receive no explicit payments. Economists refer to the costs of retaining these inputs as implicit costs. For example, an entrepreneur has alternative uses. The implicit cost of keeping an individual employed with his firm rather than with his next best alternative is the opportunity cost of his time. If he is a college graduate, this implicit cost may be quite substantial. Similarly, the foregone interest income on any savings he invests in his business is the implicit cost of those savings.

Recall that economic profits are total revenues in excess of total costs. If economic profits tend toward zero in the long run in purely competitive product markets, then producers earn total revenues sufficient to cover all costs – both explicit and implicit – but nothing in excess of that. Thus, the opportunity costs of all resources employed by all producers are being met. Because all inputs are earning an amount equal to their opportunity cost, there is no tendency for any of those resources to seek employment elsewhere. They are making a return equal to their next best alternative.

5.2 THE PURELY COMPETITIVE FIRM IN THE LONG RUN: A THIRD ASSUMPTION

Figure 5.1 (a) illustrates an equilibrium price and quantity of X. Given its short-run costs of production, at the market-determined price P, the purely competitive firm in Figure 5.1 (b) chooses to produce the quantity q, that quantity for which MR equals MC. Furthermore, this firm is making an economic profit at P because that price exceeds the average total costs (ATC) of producing q. If economic profits are characteristic of firms in this industry, what adjustment do those profits bring about?

The Purely Competitive Model in the Long Run Chapter 3 identified the two assumptions of the purely competitive model. First, there are enough producers of X so that the actions of any one producer do not affect the market supply of X, and thus its price. Second, all producers of X are

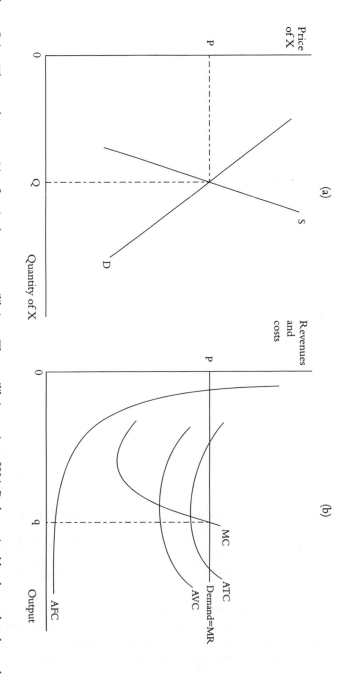

Figure 5.1 The purely competitive firm in short-run equilibrium. The equilibrium price of X is P, determined by the market demand and market supply of X, as illustrated in panel (a). At that market-determined price, the firm in panel (b) produces q, the quantity that maximizes profits. At price P, the firm is earning economic profits.

producing a homogeneous product, a product that to consumers of X is alike in all respects to the output of competing producers. These two assumptions are sufficient to generate a perfectly elastic demand for the firm's output.

The model of pure competition in the long run also contains a third assumption: there are no artificial barriers preventing the entry of new firms into the industry (or the exit of existing firms from the industry). If there exist no artificial barriers preventing the entry of new firms into an industry, when will new entrepreneurs choose to enter an industry? Entrepreneurs will choose to enter an industry when they think that it will be profitable to do so.

An Increase in the Number of Producers: A Supply Shifter   A change in the number of producers of X changes the market supply of X. In particular, an increase in the numbers of producers of X increases the market supply of X. Figure 5.2 (a) illustrates an increase in the market supply of X from S to S^*. As a consequence of this increase in market supply, the price of X falls from P to P^*. Figure 5.2 (b) illustrates the adjustment of the producer to the decrease in the price of X to P^*. In response to a fall in the price of X, this producer reduces his output from q to q^*, that quantity for which MC (which has not changed) is equal to MR^* (which has changed). Furthermore, all existing producers of X reduce their output of X. (The increase in equilibrium output in Figure 5.2 (a) from Q to Q^* is due to the output of the new producers.)

The decrease in the price of X to P^* also has another effect: it eliminates the profits of this producer. For output q^*, price P^* is equal to the average total costs (ATC) of producing that output. Furthermore, the profits of other producers of X are also reduced (if not eliminated) by the decline in the price of X. If profit-maximizing producers set out to restore their profits, what options are available to them in the long run in purely competitive product markets?

5.3   THE COSTS OF PRODUCTION IN THE LONG RUN

A purely competitive producer whose profits have disappeared cannot attempt to restore those profits by raising product price. To do so will cause his sales, thus his total revenues, to fall to zero. This constraint is placed on all producers in purely competitive product markets. However, any producer can take steps to lower the costs of production in the long run. Given a producer's total revenues, any action that reduces total costs of production will restore profits. This realization first requires an examination of the economists' concept of the long run, then an identification of those factors that permit a firm to reduce its costs in the long run.

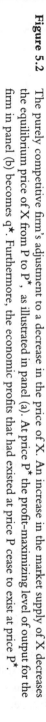

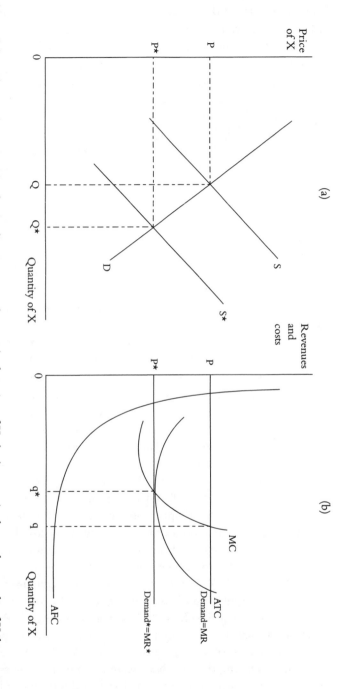

Figure 5.2   The purely competitive firm's adjustment to a decrease in the price of X. An increase in the market supply of X decreases the equilibrium price of X from P to P*, as illustrated in panel (a). At price P* the profit–maximizing level of output for the firm in panel (b) becomes q*. Furthermore, the economic profits that had existed at price P cease to exist at price P*.

The Long Run in the Theory of the Firm   The short run is that period of time during which at least one input in production cannot be changed. Thus, in the short run there is at least one fixed input; other inputs are variable. Because there are both fixed inputs and variable inputs in the short run, there are both fixed costs and variable costs in the short run. By contrast, in the long run all inputs are variable. Because all inputs are variable, all costs are variable in the long run.

It may prove helpful to think of the distinction between the short run and the long run in the following manner. Any firm assumed to maximize profits will have an incentive to adjust to a change in circumstance, a change in something external to it. Economists think that it is helpful to contrast the partial adjustments that a firm can make immediately with the full adjustments that it can make given enough time. This difference is the essential distinction between these two concepts. The short run is that period of time during which the firm can make only a partial adjustment to a change in circumstance; in the long run, a firm can fully adjust to a change in circumstance.

With these ideas in mind, consider the adjustments a producer of automobiles makes to a change in circumstance: a rise in the price of automobiles. Any profit-maximizing producer will have an incentive to increase output. In the short run, the firm will be able to make some partial adjustments immediately. For example, it can increase output by working existing workers overtime and by adding extra shifts. However, some adjustments that the firm might like to make cannot be made immediately. For example, the firm cannot change its scale of operation immediately by building a new plant to produce the extra output. Given enough time, however, the firm can build as many different-sized plants as it chooses. In the long run, all scales of operation are possible.

The firm in Figure 5.2 (b) saw its profits disappear because of the fall in the price of X from P to P^*. Given enough time, the firm can move to successively larger scales of operation if doing so will reduce its costs. Figure 5.3 illustrates a firm that does lower its average total costs by varying all of its inputs. The firm has moved from one scale of operation with short-run cost curves MC and ATC to a larger scale of operation with lower short-run cost curves MC_2 and ATC_2. Because of the firm's reductions in costs, it has expanded its output from q^* to q_2, that quantity for which MC_2 (which has now declined) is equal to MR^* (which has not changed). Furthermore, the firm's profits have been restored because product price P^* now exceeds the per-unit total costs of producing that output, ATC_2. Thus, as a result of this long-run adjustment, this firm has restored its profits by lowering its costs. All of these consequences flow from the fact that this producer has been able to lower its costs of production. Given enough time, a firm can make the following adjustments to lower its costs of production.

Adjustments that Lower Costs of Production   Any change that increases the productivity of inputs (MPP and APP) lowers the firm's costs of producing output. Productivity is a measure of output per unit input. Some individuals confuse the concept of productivity with that of production. Production is merely a measure of output. Measures of productivity require two variables: inputs and outputs. Perhaps the most common measure of productivity is output per worker-hour. What would cause output per worker-hour to rise?

1. An increase in the quantity of other inputs with which labor works will increase the productivity of workers. Given enough time, a firm can increase the amounts of capital, land, and other inputs labor uses in production. In the case of capital, some of the addition to this stock of productive capacity is embodied in workers in the form of education.

2. An improvement in technology will increase the productivity of work-

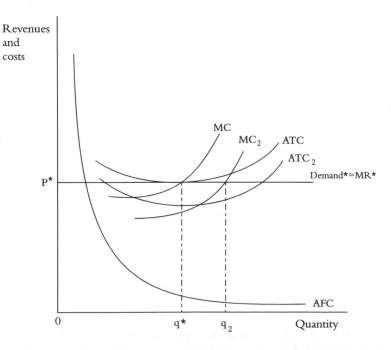

Figure 5.3   Restoration of economic profits. Given costs ATC and MC, this firm produces q* at price P* and earns no economic profits. By lowering its costs to ATC_2 and MC_2, the firm can restore its profits.

ers. It is helpful to think of technology as the technique of production, the means by which inputs are transformed into outputs. Conceptually speaking, it is easy to disentangle the techniques by which inputs are transformed into outputs from the phenomenon mentioned in item 1, an increase in the quantities of inputs. Practically speaking, however, new techniques are often embodied in new capital and other inputs. What this means practically is that it is sometimes hard to disentangle and measure that portion of an improvement in productivity due to an improvement in technology from that portion due to an increase in the quantity of inputs employed.

3. Given the productivity of inputs, a decline in the price of an input lowers the costs of producing output. In constructing a producer's long-run average total cost curve, prices of inputs are taken as given. (Changes in the price of an input will shift the long-run cost schedule.)

The Long-Run Average Total Cost Curve   How can adjustments in the firm's scale of operations be described as a decline in long-run costs when the firm has simply moved from one short-run scale of operation to another? Recall how the long run is conceptualized in the theory of the firm. Enough time is allowed for the firm to make whatever adjustment it wants to a change in circumstance. In this case, the change in circumstance has been adverse: the price of the product it sells has declined, thus eliminating its profits. Given enough time to make whatever adjustments it chooses to, the firm has chosen to move to a larger scale of operation with the lower cost curves MC_2 and ATC_2. Yet, when the firm has made whatever adjustments it wishes to make to become more efficient, it finds itself once again in the short run. Thus, while it is correct to say that all producers can make whatever adjustments they wish to lower costs, given enough time to do so, it is also correct to say that all producers are in the short run at any given moment.

Any cost relation connects two variables: costs and output. Thus, the long-run average total cost curve (LRATC) is an envelope curve that connects minimum short-run average total costs (SRATC) with the associated levels of ouput in alternative scales of operation. The LRATC curve illustrates how a firm's minimum average total costs would vary if it were to move through time to successively larger scales of operation. Figure 5.4 illustrates a long-run average total cost curve. If it continued to move to successively larger scales of operation, this firm would experience declining average total costs of production until the plant size with SRATC" was reached.

The cost reductions that a firm experiences by becoming larger are called *economies of scale*. The term is a shorthand way of stating that there may be cost reductions (economies) possible with larger scales of operation. Notice, however, that the firm's average total costs rise if the firm expands its scale of operation beyond that plant size with SRATC". A firm at some scale of operation might not be able to lower its per-unit total costs by becoming larger. It might instead experience diseconomies of scale. Why might a firm's costs rise (not fall) by becoming larger? Costs might rise because of problems of coordination and control. Firms often become increasingly bureaucratic as they get larger. They add layers of management, and those additional layers of managers not merely add to the firm's payroll costs but also raise the costs of communication within the firm. If a firm experiences diseconomies of scale, then its LRATC begins to rise.

The economies of scale that are available to firms in any given industry

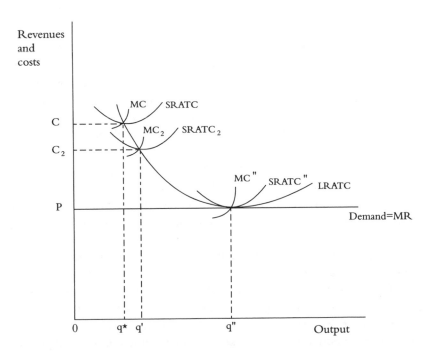

Figure 5.4   Costs and economic profits in the long run in purely competitive product markets. The long-run average total cost curve (LRATC) illustrates how a firm's minimum average total costs would vary if it moved through time to successively larger scales of operation. Because firms are free to enter an industry in the purely competitive model, product price will tend toward the minimum average total cost in the long run in that model. Thus, economic profits will tend toward zero in the long run for purely competitive producers.

may be exhausted quickly. In that event, the industry will be characterized by a relatively large number of relatively small firms (even in purely competitive product markets). By contrast, industries in which economies of scale are substantial will tend to be characterized by a relatively small number of relatively large firms (even in purely competitive product markets).

5.4   REACHING THE CONCLUSION

In purely competitive product markets, producers are forced to move toward their most efficient scale of operation if they expect to survive in the long run. In Figure 5.4, this producer's most efficient scale of operation is the plant size with SRATC". What are the full implications of this conclusion for consumers of X? What precise market forces are responsible for this conclusion?

When the firm in Figure 5.3 acts to lower its per-unit total costs, that cost reduction does restore its profits. However, this improvement in the profitability of existing producers is strictly temporary. If the firms in the industry have regained profitability, then that profitability again attracts new producers. As before, the entry of the new firms increases the market supply of X. The increase in the market supply of X decreases the equilibrium price of X. The decrease in the price of X again erodes (and ultimately eliminates) the economic profits of the firms in the industry.

The producers of X can restore profits by moving yet again to a lower-cost scale of operation if economies of scale are possible. That adjustment again restores profitability, but again those newly regained profits are temporary. Thus, the logic of this argument is inescapable. All producers in purely competitive product markets are forced through time to move toward that scale of operation at which their per-unit total costs are at a minimum. If they refuse to do so, they do not survive.

In Figure 5.4 the scale of operation at which this firm's per-unit total costs are at a minimum is that plant size with SRATC". Because MR is price in purely competitive markets, the price of any good X tends in the long run in purely competitive product markets toward the minimum cost of producing that good. This is the conclusion we set out to reach at the beginning of Part I; this is the conclusion we have now reached.

5.5   PURE COMPETITION AND YOUR UTILITY

Given your money income, a fall in the prices of the goods and services that you consume increases your real income. Because real income is the variable that constrains your consumption, you are now able to attain higher quantities of the goods you consume. Because your total utility varies directly with the quantities of goods that you consume, your total utility increases as a result of ever decreasing product prices through time. Furthermore, economists have been successful in demonstrating that, for the society as a whole, total output (and welfare) tends toward its maximum in purely competitive markets.

The increase in your consumption and utility is not due to the benevolence of producers. Nonetheless, in the course of pursuing their own interests, producers cause the level of your utility to rise. This conclusion follows logically when producers pursue their own interests by means of exchange in purely competitive product markets. The purely competitive model harnesses the self-interest-seeking propensities of producers in such a way that they benefit consumers, not producers.

That there exist no artificial barriers preventing new firms from entering an industry if they choose to is the assumption that ensures the conclusion that product price tends toward minimum LRATC. It would be impossible to reach the conclusion in this chapter without this assumption. It is the entry of new firms that increases the market supply of X, decreasing the price of X, and eroding the economic profits of producers of X, forcing them to become more efficient over time. Because it is precisely this assumption that guarantees the conclusion that economic profits in all purely competitive markets will tend toward zero, it is not at all unexpected that, in some actual product markets, existing producers will pursue their own interests by attempting to block the entry of new producers into their industries. The methods that existing producers employ to block the entry of new firms into existing industries is the subject of Chapter 6. There we will also see how consumers lose as a consequence of these self-interest-seeking activities of producers.

5.6 QUESTIONS

1. Is it possible that your accountant might tell you that you were making an economic profit in your new restaurant, while at the same time and with the same information an economist would advise you to close down?
2. Does it make any difference in the analysis in this chapter if the new entrant into the industry is a foreign rather than a domestic firm?
3. Unions bargain for higher wages in a manufacturing plant in Ohio, while at the same time resisting changes in work rules that would

increase productivity. What adjustments can this firm make (a) in the short run and (b) in the long run?

4. As a firm becomes larger it can more readily specialize in production. How does the specialization of labor lead to a decrease in the costs of production?

5. As you have seen in this chapter, there are inexorable tendencies toward efficiency in purely competitive product markets. But it is also true that price equals marginal cost in these markets. What is the significance of this equality?

6

Monopoly and Rent-Seeking Activity
in Product Markets

The purely competitive model contains two common assumptions in both its short-run and long-run versions. First, there are enough producers of good X so that the actions of any one producer of X (to expand output or to leave the industry, for example) do not affect the market supply of X and, therefore, the price of X. Each firm in a purely competitive product market is a price taker. Second, each firm is producing a homogeneous output, a product that consumers view as alike in all respects to the output of the other firms in the industry. These two assumptions are sufficient to generate the conclusion in purely competitive product markets that the demand for each firm's output is perfectly elastic at the market-determined price.

These two assumptions can also be interpreted from the point of view of consumers of X. The first assumption confronts consumers of X with the widest possible array of options in consumption: all the firms that produce X. Furthermore, from the point of view of consumers, there is no reason whatsoever to prefer the output of one firm over the output of any other firm in the industry; to consumers, all producers of X are producing an identical product. Keeping in mind the determinants of elasticity of demand for any product, this second interpretation presents individual demanders of X with the widest possible array of perfect substitutes in consumption. From this perspective also, the demand for the output of each producer will be perfectly elastic.

Because the purely competitive model presents each consumer with the widest possible array of perfect substitutes in consumption, that model is a limit (or polar) case. It is possible to construct another limit case that is as far removed from the purely competitive model as possible. This other limit-case

73

model is monopoly. Economists argue that if you are required to purchase goods and services from a monopolist, you will attain lower levels of total utility than you would in purely competitive markets. Section 6.1 presents the model of monopoly; we will see exactly how you become worse off when you confront a monopolist in a product market.

The third assumption of the purely competitive model is a long-run consideration: new producers are free to enter an industry if they choose to. In Chapter 5, we found that the price consumers pay for the various goods and services they consume will tend, over time, in purely competitive product markets toward their minimum per-unit total costs of production. However, if existing producers are successful in preventing the entry of new producers into their industry, no such conclusion follows. All those efforts designed to block (or otherwise restrict) the entry of new firms into industries are *rent-seeking* activities. Existing producers benefit from rent-seeking activities; however, they benefit at the expense of consumers. The analysis of rent-seeking activities by producers is also presented in this chapter.

6.1 MONOPOLY

The monopoly model contains assumptions that result in each individual's confronting the smallest possible array of options in consumption. These assumptions are best understood by contrasting them with the assumptions of the purely competitive model.

The Assumptions of Monopoly　　In the monopoly model, there is one assumption that there is only one seller of X and a second assumption that there are no close substitutes for X. Thus, the monopolist is the one seller of a product or service that has no close substitutes. Whereas the purely competitive model presents each individual with the widest possible array of options in consumption, the monopoly model deliberately constructs the opposite set of circumstances: each individual confronts the smallest possible array of options in consumption. You purchase X from the one seller of X or you do without. (It is important to stress that the monopoly model is not a model of coercion. Consumers are not required or forced to purchase X from the one seller of X. Rather, the model is one in which individuals who pursue their own objectives in society by means of exchange confront the smallest possible array of options in exchange.) These two assumptions of the monopoly model are sufficient to generate a relatively inelastic demand for the monopolist's output.

There is a third assumption in the monopoly model. In the purely competitive model, new firms are permitted to enter an industry and do so if profits are characteristic of that industry. In the monopoly model, there are barriers that prevent the entry of new firms into the industry. If this assumption were not in force, the one-firm model of monopoly would quickly collapse.

Before beginning the formal analysis of monopoly, some common misperceptions about the monopolist should be addressed. For example, it is common to imagine that the monopolist is a large producer. There is no reason to think of a monopolist as a large firm; the single cello teacher in a small town comes closer to the monopoly model than does General Motors. Second, it is sometimes said that because the monopolist is the sole producer of X, it can charge any price it wants to for X. This, too, is an error. Based on their incomes, tastes, and other determinants of demand, consumers determine the maximum price they are willing to pay for various quantities of X. Third, many people tend to think that monopolists always make profits. This conclusion does not follow logically from the monopoly model either. Just because a firm is the sole producer of cast-iron stoves does not imply that it can sell those stoves at prices that exceed its per-unit total costs of production. Try to put these misperceptions aside and think instead about individuals pursuing their objectives in society by means of exchange in a particular set of circumstances: they confront the smallest imaginable number of options in exchange.

The Demand for the Monopolist's Output   In Figure 6.1 (a), the interaction of the market demand for X and the market supply of X determines the equilibrium price of X. At this price, P, the purely competitive firm in Figure 6.1 (b) can sell all the output that it chooses to. Because the demand for its output is perfectly elastic, its product price is also this producer's marginal revenue (MR) and its average revenue (AR).

What would the demand for this producer's output be if it became a monopolist instead of a purely competitive producer of X? The schedule that illustrates the market quantities demanded of X at various alternative prices of X is the market demand for X, the schedule labelled D in Figure 6.1 (a). Because there is only one firm producing X in the monopoly model, this schedule becomes the demand for the monopolist's output.

The Marginal Revenue Schedule for the Monopolist   Figure 6.2 illustrates this demand for the monpolist's output. This producer of X can sell additional quantities of X, but only by lowering the price of X. Thus, if the price of X were $1.00, then the firm could sell 10 units of X. By doing so,

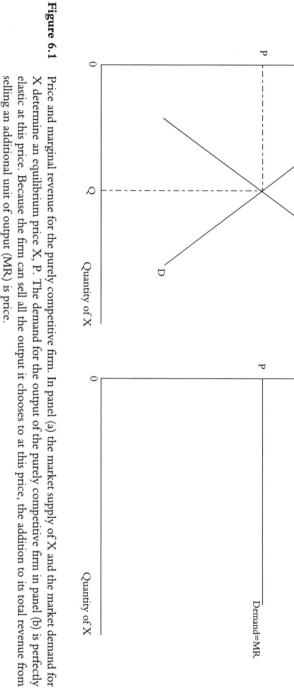

Figure 6.1   Price and marginal revenue for the purely competitive firm. In panel (a) the market supply of X and the market demand for X determine an equilibrium price X, P. The demand for the output of the purely competitive firm in panel (b) is perfectly elastic at this price. Because the firm can sell all the output it chooses to at this price, the addition to its total revenue from selling an additional unit of output (MR) is price.

its total revenues would be $10.00. If, on the other hand, the price were $.95, then this producer could sell 11 units of X. Its total revenues from selling 11 units of X at $.95 would be $10.45. What, then, is the change in the firm's total revenues from selling 11 units at $.95 instead of 10 at $1.00? For the monopolist, the marginal revenue of the 11th unit of output is $.45, less than the price at which the 11th unit can be sold ($.95). Furthermore, there is nothing unique about the 11th unit of output. For every quantity of X, marginal revenue will be less than the price at which that quantity can be sold. Thus, in Figure 6.2 there is a separate marginal revenue schedule (MR) for the monopolist, a schedule that lies below and falls faster than the demand schedule.

Marginal revenue can be negative. If some given percentage price reduction leads to a smaller percentage increase in the sales of output, then total revenue will decrease. This would be the case if the demand for the product were

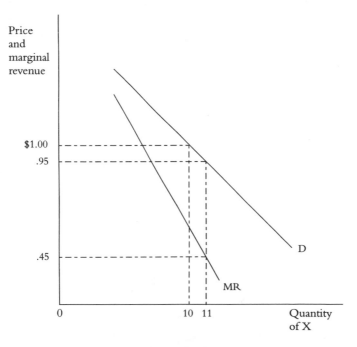

Figure 6.2   Price and marginal revenue for the monopolist. The demand for the monopolist's output is D. If product price were $1.00, then the monopolist could sell 10 units of output; if product price were $.95, then it could sell 11 units of output. The addition to total revenue from selling 11 rather than 10 units of output (MR) is $.45, an amount lower than the price at which 11 units of output can be sold: $.95. Thus, marginal revenue is less than price for each quantity of output.

inelastic. No profit-maximizing producer would ever knowingly lower its product price if the demand for its product were inelastic; by doing so, its total revenues would fall.

The Profit-Maximizing Monopolist   Like any other firm, the monopolist is assumed to maximize profits. There is nothing different about the decision rule that the monopolist follows in maximizing its profits: it produces that quantity for which the addition to total revenues from selling the output (MR) is equal to the addition to total costs from producing it (MC). Given the cost and revenue schedules in Figure 6.3, that is the quantity q.

The monopolist, however, has a second decision to make, a decision that the purely competitive firm did not have to make. In the purely competitive model, there was a market-determined price, and the purely competitive firm simply decided what quantity to sell at that price. The monopolist, however, confronts no market-determined price. Thus, the monopolist must choose the price that it will charge for output q. Is there a schedule that illustrates

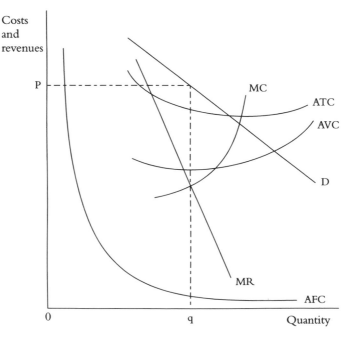

Figure 6.3   The monopolist's choice of output and price. Given the monopolist's cost and revenue schedules, the profit-maximizing level of output is q. For that quantity, the monopolist charges the maximum price that consumers are willing to pay: P.

the maximum price that consumers are willing to pay for the quantity q? Yes, there is. The demand schedule always provides this information. Thus, the monopolist will charge the price P, the maximum price that consumers are willing to pay for the quantity q. Although this producer is making a profit at price P (P exceeds ATC for the quantity q), profitability is not a necessary conclusion of the monopoly model.

It is possible to show the loss from monopoly in two different ways. First, at any price, the monopolist will produce less output than will the purely competitive firm with the same costs. Second, for any quantity, the monopolist will charge a higher price than will the purely competitive firm with the same costs. Consider these propositions in turn.

Less Output at Every Price

Less Output at Every Price   The monopolist will produce less output at every price than will the purely competitive firm with the same costs. The firm in Figure 6.4 is first presented as a monopolist with its short-run costs. Its demand schedule is D; its marginal revenue schedule is MR. Given its short-run costs, the monopolist produces output q and sells it for the price P (as in Figure 6.3). Now, let this monopolist (with these costs) become a purely competitive firm. If this firm with these costs were a purely competitive firm selling output at price P, then its demand schedule would be perfectly elastic at that price (Demand* in Figure 6.4). Furthermore, Demand* would also be its marginal revenue and average revenue schedule. This firm would not produce and sell the output q with these new revenue schedules, however. It would produce and sell a larger amount of output, q_C, that quantity for which MR* equals MC. Furthermore, the same is true for other prices as well. Thus, the monopolist produces less output at every price than does the purely competitive firm with the same costs. This reduced output is one cost to consumers who purchase from monopolists.

Higher Prices for Every Quantity

Higher Prices for Every Quantity   It is also possible to show that the monopolist will charge a higher price for every quantity of output than will the purely competitive firm with the same costs. Figure 6.5 illustrates again the monopolist with demand schedule D and marginal revenue schedule MR producing the profit-maximizing output q for which it charges the price P_M. Can one say what price consumers would have paid for this output q had it been produced by a purely competitive firm with these same costs? Yes, for if this firm had been a purely competitive firm producing q, marginal revenue would be equal to marginal cost for this quantity. Thus, price P_C would be this firm's marginal revenue. Again, there is nothing unusual about this particular price and quantity. For each quantity, the purely competitive firm will charge a lower price. Thus, a second cost of monopoly to consumers is a higher price for each and every quantity of output.

If one asked individuals who had no training in economics whether they would be better off with a wider or a narrower array of options in consumption, they probably without exception would choose wider. That common-sense conclusion holds here in this formal analysis as well. Measured either in less output or in higher prices, consumers do pay a price when their options in consumption are reduced. In the monopoly model, those options are reduced to the minimum.

It is entirely possible that the one seller of a product or service that has no close substitutes may emerge temporarily in product markets. This emergence could be due to a new product or a new idea. For some period of time, then, consumers of that good would indeed confront no close substitutes in consumption. If the one producer is profitable, however, other producers will

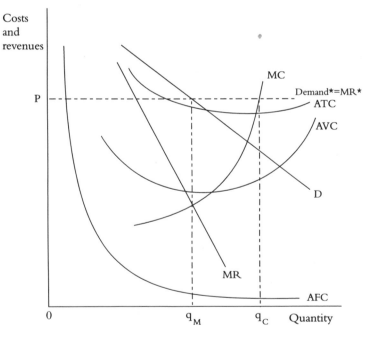

Figure 6.4   Less output at every price. Given its cost and revenue schedules the monopolist chooses to produce q_M and charge the price P. Had this firm been a purely competitive producer, its demand (Demand*) would have been perfectly elastic at price P, and it would have produced q_C at that price (given its costs). Thus, the monopolist produces less output at every price than does the purely competitive firm with the same costs.

choose to enter that one-firm industry and produce similar (if not identical) outputs. As one firm becomes two, and two become three, the industry grows over time as long as producers are profitable and there are no barriers to the entry of new producers. Thus, the one firm ceases to be a monopolist over time. However, profits in an industry can be artificially supported by certain specific rent-seeking activities of producers.

6.2 RENT-SEEKING ACTIVITY BY PRODUCERS

In Chapter 5, we saw how the self-interest-seeking activities of producers led, through no intent of their own, to increases in the welfare of consumers over time. In particular, the prices consumers pay for the various goods and

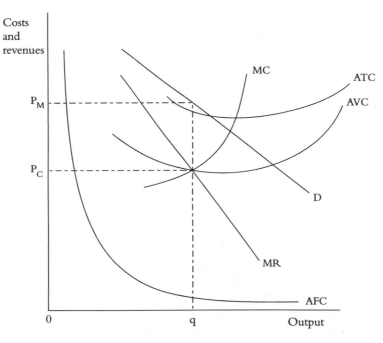

Figure 6.5 Higher prices for every quantity. Given its revenue and cost schedules, the monopolist chooses to produce q and charge the price P_M. Had this firm been a purely competitive firm producing q, the addition to its total costs from producing that quantity would have been equal to the addition to its total revenues from doing so: MC = MR for output q. Because MR is equal to price for the purely competitive firm, that firm would have charged P_C for this level of output. Thus, for any level of output, the monopolist charges a higher price than does the purely competitive firm with the same costs.

services they consume will tend, in the long run, toward the minimum per-unit total costs of production in purely competitive product markets. This conclusion follows from a specific assumption in that model: there are no artificial barriers that prevent new firms from entering industries.

This conclusion is equivalent to saying that in purely competitive product markets, economic profits of producers tend toward zero. It is precisely because new firms are allowed to enter industries, thus increasing product supply and decreasing product price, that this conclusion follows logically. Although consumers benefit from this product–market structure, producers clearly do not benefit. Furthermore, producers, whom we assume strive to maximize profits, will have an incentive to take a variety of steps designed to prevent this conclusion from occurring. Every particular tactic that producers can think to employ, however, has one overriding strategy: block completely (or at least impede) the entry of new producers into the industry. Every such activity designed to block or impede the entry of new firms into existing industries is a rent-seeking activity.

The concept of *rent* is one that originates in the market for land, and is presented in detail in Chapter 11. Rather than detour here for a full presentation of that concept, note for the present that in the terminology used here, rent is a portion of a price. To illustrate this concept, consider the automobile industry. If automobiles were actually produced in an industry where there were no artificial barriers to entry, then the actual price of automobiles, P_A, would tend toward the competitive price of automobiles, P_C. However, because automobiles are actually produced in an industry in which substantial barriers to entry exist, the actual price of automobiles exceeds the competitive price of automobiles: $P_A > P_C$. Rent is the amount by which P_A exceeds P_C. Rent, then, is an element (or a portion) of the actual price, P_A.

If rent-seeking activity is successful, product price is higher than it otherwise would be. Given the costs of production, higher product prices increase the firm's profits. Thus, rent-seeking activity is yet another means that producers can employ to increase their profits. Unlike lowering their costs of production, however, this activity yields no benefits to consumers. Note, nonetheless, that for producers this activity may be a low-cost substitute for lowering costs over time.

One does not expect producers in industry Z to state publicly that they are pursuing their own interests in their efforts to block the entry of new producers into their industry. And this expectation is realized. What excuse do producers offer for their efforts to block the entry of other producers into their industry? The usual answer is "to protect jobs." But if because of higher prices in industry Z, consumers have less income to spend on the output of industries A through Y, won't employment in industries A through Y be less than it otherwise would be? Won't the maintained employment in industry Z be at the expense of less employment in other industries in the economy? Yes, it would. But producers in an industry can often get a sympathetic ear when they use this excuse, particularly when the new producers that seek to enter an industry are foreign producers.

How can existing producers block the entry of new producers into an industry? There are some means that are explicit and widely understood by virtually everyone in society. Such tactics as lobbying politicians for higher tariffs, import duties, and quotas on goods produced by foreign producers are standard examples of overt means that employers can use in their search for rents. Some means, however, often escape the eye of the public or are misunderstood. Consider but one of these many possibilities.

Assume that your college degree is in communications, and that you and your friends want to open a new television station in the United States when you graduate. What is to prevent your doing so? A federal regulatory agency, the Federal Communications Commission (FCC), prevents your doing so. When the FCC blocks the entry of new firms into an industry, whose interests are being served? Regulatory agencies are suppliers of regulation. What the economic theory of regulation concludes is that actions to control entry into an industry are designed to respond to the demanders of regulation: existing firms in an industry. Thus, what the economic theory of regulation concludes is that regulatory agencies do not always (or even usually) protect consumers from large firms. Rather, regulatory agencies usually protect existing firms in an industry from the competition of new suppliers. Thus, a less obvious form of self-interest-seeking behavior by producers is seeking protection from regulatory agencies.

6.3 QUESTIONS

1. Common estimates of the welfare loss to Americans from monopoly are about $2.00 per person per year. Do you find this estimate surprising? Why?

2. For whatever reasons, individuals are reluctant to admit that they pursue their own interests through their actions. Thus, we must endure explanations as to how their actions will benefit us. How exactly are we to benefit from self-seeking activities of the auto producers that result in cars in the United States costing about $2,000 more than they otherwise would?

3. How is the distribution of income in the United States affected by rent-seeking activities of auto producers that raise the price of cars an average of $2,000?

PART
── II ──

Pure Competition and Equality: Factor Markets

When we shift our attention from product markets to factor markets, the role of producers and consumers is reversed. Producers who are suppliers of goods and services in product markets are demanders of inputs in markets for factors of production. Similarly, household members who are demanders of goods and services in product markets are suppliers of factors of production in factor markets.

Throughout the discussion of factor markets in Part II, the prices of goods and services that individuals consume are taken as given. Given the prices of the goods and services you consume, your real income will be higher, the higher your money income. Your money income is the sum of two component parts: nonlabor income and labor income. Nonlabor income is income that you receive independent of any hours that you work. Labor income (Y) is the product of two variables: the wage (W) at which you work multiplied by the hours (H) that you work: $Y = (W) (H)$.

In Chapter 7, we again construct the theory of producer choice. But this time we extend the implications of that theory into the labor market in order to reach the following conclusion: labor demand. You discover that the wage workers receive in purely competitive labor markets tends toward their contribution to the firm's total revenues, the maximum amount that a profit-maximizing firm is willing to pay. Thus, given your skills, the wage at which you work tends toward its maximum in purely competitive labor markets.

In Chapter 8, we construct the theory of consumer choice, but we extend that theory into the labor market in order to reach the following conclusion: labor supply. We see that the quantity of labor that an individual chooses to supply is a function of the wage. Because household members are assumed to be utility maximizers, they may choose to work fewer hours at higher wages. One implication of this conclusion is immediate and important: a portion of the actual distribution of incomes across households in purely competitive labor markets is chosen.

There are inexorable tendencies toward equality of outcomes in purely competitive labor markets. In particular, average real wages for like types of labor tend toward equality across both industries and regions. Chapter 9 identifies those market forces that determine an equilibrium wage for an occupation and specifies those factors that cause an equilibrium wage to change. In Chapter 10, we reach the conclusion that average real wages for any given occupation will tend toward equality across both industries and regions in purely competitive labor markets. Thus, given their skills, individuals cannot, on average, increase the wage that they earn by changing industries or regions.

Through various types of rent-seeking activities, self-interest-seeking individuals may be able to reduce the options available to workers in labor markets and thus impede these tendencies toward equality of outcomes for like types of labor. Chapter 11 presents the model of monopsony and explains how the rent-seeking activities of occupational groups can alter the purely competitive conclusion so as to gain an element of rent in their occupational wage.

Chapter 12 concludes the discussion of factor markets by presenting the elements of capital theory. In this chapter, we discover that individuals can increase the wage at which they can work by making human capital investments in themselves.

7

Labor Demand: A Conclusion of the Theory of Producer Choice

This chapter leads to a most important conclusion: the wage that workers earn in purely competitive labor markets will be the maximum amount that profit-maximizing firms are willing to pay. Any schedule that illustrates the maximum price that a demander of X will be willing to pay for various quantities of X is a demand schedule. Thus, in order to reach this conclusion it becomes necessary to derive the firm's demand for labor.

Beginning from the hypothesis of profit maximization, we constructed the theory of producer choice in Chapter 3 and found that product supply was a conclusion of that theory. Beginning from the same hypothesis as before, we will extend the theory of producer choice into the labor market in order to reach a conclusion there: labor demand. Because we are already familiar with this theory, our task here becomes somewhat easier.

7.1 LABOR DEMAND DEFINED

Figure 7.1 illustrates a firm's demand for labor. The independent variable, the wage rate, is on the vertical axis. The dependent variable, quantity demanded of labor, is on the horizontal axis. As before, demand is subject to two equally valid interpretations. In one interpretation, this schedule is a series of "if, then" statements. *If* the wage rate were W, *then* this firm would choose to employ the quantity Q of labor. *If*, on the other hand, the wage rate were to decrease to W*, *then* this firm would change its behavior: it would increase the employment of labor to Q*. Thus, the relation between these two variables is negative.

Alternatively, this schedule illustrates the maximum price that this firm would be willing to pay for various quantities of labor. The maximum price that it is willing to pay for the quantity Q is W. The maximum price the firm is willing to pay for the larger quantity Q^* is a lower maximum wage, W^*. Thus, the maximum wage that a profit-maximizing producer is willing to pay labor decreases as the quantity employed of labor increases.

The objective here is to derive a schedule that will satisfy these two interpretations, for any such schedule is by definition a demand schedule. Because the firm in economic theory is the producing unit, you must necessarily redirect your attention to the theory of production. Although the input–output relations are engineeering relations and thus of no interest to economists in and of themselves, they become interesting because production relations have implications for the firm's demand for labor (and other factors of production).

7.2 PRODUCTION RELATIONS

In Chapter 3, we observed that a producer of brooms could produce any given quantity of brooms using various combinations of inputs of labor and

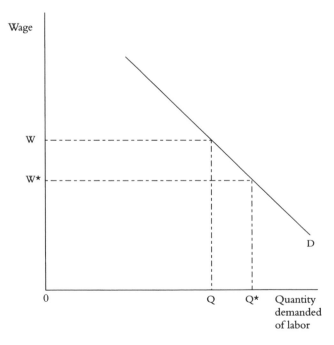

Figure 7.1   The demand for labor. The firm's demand for labor is a negative relation between the wage rate (the independent variable) and the quantity demanded of labor (the dependent variable).

capital. An isoquant illustrates all such combinations that produce equal quantities of output. To produce increased quantities of brooms requires more labor (no less capital), more capital (no less labor), or more of both inputs. Figure 7.2 reproduces Figure 3.2 and illustrates a "family" of such isoquants for a producer of brooms.

Given enough time, a firm can alter the employment of all of its inputs and will, in purely competitive product markets, tend to produce its output in the most efficient manner. In the short run, however, the firm can only make partial adjustments to a change in circumstance. Place this producer in the short run by fixing the employment of capital at three units ($K^* = 3$), and raise the question: how can this producer of brooms increase output when its capital is fixed at three units? The answer, of course, is that this producer uses more of the factor that can be increased – labor. Figure 7.3 (a) illustrates how

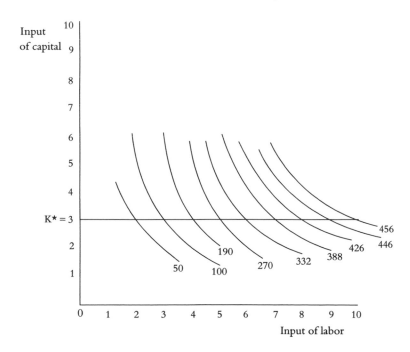

Figure 7.2   Production relations. This figure is a reproduction of Figure 3.2. Any given quantity of output can be produced using various combinations of inputs. The isoquants here illustrate various combinations of capital and labor that can be employed to produce equal quantities of brooms. If the input of capital were fixed at three units, then increases in the output of brooms could be accomplished only by increasing the input that is not fixed–labor.

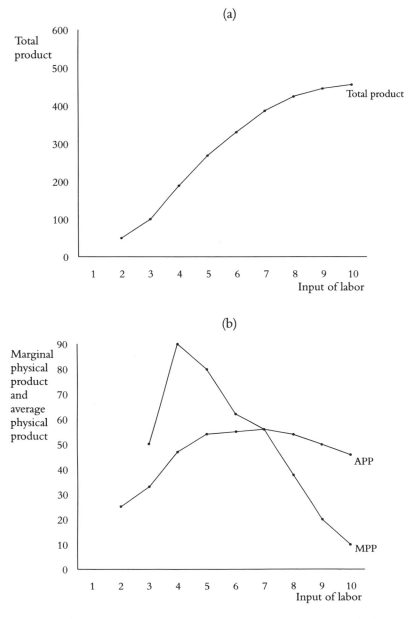

Figure 7.3 Total product, marginal product, and average product in the short run. This figure reproduces Figure 3.3. In the short run, increases in the input of labor increase the total product (output) of brooms as illustrated in panel (a). Panel (b) illustrates diminishing marginal returns in production, as well as the relationship of marginal physical product to average physical product.

total product increases as a firm increases the employment of labor and keeps capital at a fixed amount. Figure 7.3 (b) illustrates both the marginal physical product and average physical product of labor in this production process. Again, note that diminishing returns in production are characteristic of this production process in the short run. Beginning with the fifth worker, all subsequent workers add positive (but diminishing) additions to the firm's output. As you will discover shortly, diminishing returns in production have important implications for the firm's demand for labor in the short run.

7.3   ONE INTERPRETATION OF THE DEMAND FOR LABOR

Now go one step beyond these input–output relations and raise the question: how does the firm's total revenue increase by hiring additional inputs of labor? This is a concept known as the value of the marginal physical product, VMPP. The value of the marginal physical product of labor is defined as the change in the firm's total revenue (dTR) from hiring an additional input of labor (dL): VMPP = dTR/dL. You have solved one piece of that puzzle, because you now know that by hiring the fifth worker, for example, the firm's output of brooms increases by 80. How does one go from 80 brooms to a change in revenue? Firms accomplish this by selling the brooms.

How does the firm's total revenue change as it sells additional brooms? The answer to that question depends on the type of product market in which the firm sells its brooms. If the firm sells brooms in purely competitive product markets, then the change in the firm's total revenue from selling brooms is product price. Thus, if the price of brooms in purely competitive product markets is $2.00, then MR is $2.00.

In Section 7.2, we connected logically the increase in the employment of labor with an increase in the output of brooms (MPP). We can now connect logically the increase in the employment of labor with an increase in total revenues by multiplying MPP by the change in the firm's total revenues from selling the brooms (MR). The product of these two variables is the VMPP of labor. Thus, for example, the amount by which the firm's total output increases from hiring the fifth worker (MPP) is 80 brooms. If the amount by which the firm's total revenue increases from selling additional brooms (MR) is $2.00, then the change in the firm's total revenue from hiring the fifth worker is $160.00. Table 7.1 presents the VMPP of workers employed in the production of brooms, assuming a product price of $2.00.

No firm assumed to maximize profits would ever knowingly pay a worker a wage higher than the amount by which its total revenues increase by hiring

Table 7.1

Input of labor	Total product	Marginal physical product	Marginal revenue	Value of the marginal physical product
2	50			
3	100	50	$2.00	$100.00
4	190	90	2.00	180.00
5	270	80	2.00	160.00
6	332	62	2.00	124.00
7	388	56	2.00	112.00
8	426	38	2.00	76.00
9	446	20	2.00	40.00
10	456	10	2.00	20.00

The value of the marginal physical product of labor. The increase in the firm's total revenue from hiring additional inputs (VMPP) is the MPP of labor multiplied by marginal revenue.

the worker (the VMPP of the worker). Because one interpretation of a demand schedule for labor is a schedule showing the maximum price the firm will pay for various quantities of labor, the VMPP schedule satisfies this first interpretation. Thus, the schedule of VMPP is the firm's demand for labor.

Note how diminishing returns in production make themselves felt again in the theory of producer choice. A declining schedule of VMPP for labor in the short run illustrates that a profit-maximizing producer will be willing to increase the employment of labor in the short run, but only at lower wages. Why does this schedule of the VMPP of labor have a negative slope in the short run? The reason is diminishing returns in production: additional workers add fewer and fewer brooms to the firm's total output of brooms. The downward slope of the VMPP schedule in the short run in purely competitive product markets is due solely to diminishing returns in production.

7.4   A SECOND INTERPRETATION OF THE DEMAND FOR LABOR

There is a second interpretation of demand: the demand for labor is also a series of "if, then" statements. Thus, if the wage were $160.00 (per unit time), then the firm would choose to hire five workers. The VMPP schedule can also satisfy this second interpretation of demand; however, it is necessary to extend the discussion to see why.

Marginal Factor Cost in Purely Competitive Labor Markets   In Section 7.3, the firm sells its output in purely competitive product markets. In what type of labor market does the firm hire its labor? Just because one assumes that the firm is selling its output in purely competitive product markets implies nothing about the type of labor market in which it buys its labor. Assume in this discussion that the firm is buying labor in purely competitive labor markets.

Recall the two assumptions of the purely competitive model in the product market. First, there are enough firms so that the actions of any one firm do not affect the market supply of output and, therefore, the price of output. In other words, each firm takes product–selling price as a given, determined in the market. Second, all firms are selling a homogeneous product, a product that is alike in all respects to the output of other producers. These two assumptions together are sufficient to generate a perfectly elastic demand for the firm's output at the market-determined price in purely competitive product markets.

Now adapt these two assumptions to the labor market. First, there are enough firms so that the actions of any one firm do not affect the market demand for labor and, therefore, the wage rate. Each firm takes the wage rate as given, determined external to the firm in the market for labor. Second, all labor is homogeneous. Thus, there is no reason for a firm to prefer one input to another; all workers in the occupational labor market are alike in all respects. These two assumptions taken together are sufficient to generate a perfectly elastic supply of labor at the market-determined wage to each firm in purely competitive labor markets.

Figure 7.4 (a) illustrates an equilibrium market wage, $160.00, determined in an occupational labor market. Figure 7.4 (b) illustrates a perfectly elastic supply of labor to the firm at that wage. If the firm can hire all the labor that it wishes to at $160.00 per unit time, what is marginal factor cost (MFC) to the firm? MFC is the amount by which the firm's total costs change (dTC) from hiring additional workers (dL): MFC = dTC/dL. If the firm can hire all the labor that it wishes to at $160.00 per unit time, then its MFC is a constant equal to the wage – in this case, $160.

One Wage, One Quantity   There is now enough information to allow this firm to make an employment decision. Table 7.1 presented the amount by which this firm's total revenue changes from hiring additional inputs of labor – the VMPP of workers. Now it is known how much the firm's total costs change from hiring additional inputs of labor – the MFC of workers. A firm assumed to maximize profits will hire all inputs that add more to its

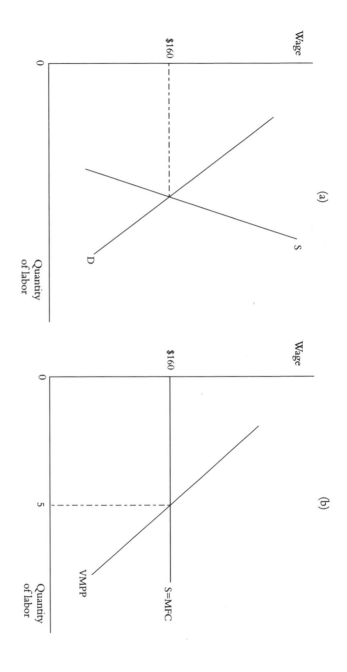

Figure 7.4   One wage, one quantity. The market wage of $160 is determined in the market for labor. If the firm is purely competitive in its labor market, then the supply of labor to the firm is perfectly elastic at the market wage, and the addition to its total costs from hiring an additional worker (MFC) is the wage: $160. The profit-maximizing firm hires five workers, the quantity for which VMPP = MFC.

total revenues than to its total costs (that is, all workers for whom VMPP > MFC) and will hire no workers that add more to its total costs than to its total revenues (that is, no workers for whom MFC > VMPP). Given the schedules of VMPP and MFC, the quantity of labor that maximizes the firm's profits is five workers, that quantity for which VMPP = MFC. Thus, *if* the wage were $160.00, *then* the firm would hire five workers.

However, the demand for labor is a series of "if, then" statements. Accordingly, it is necessary to present this producer with an alternative price of labor.

Reaching the Conclusion   In Figure 7.5 (a), the market supply of labor increases from S to S*, so that the market wage rate decreases to $124 (per unit time). At that new market wage, the supply of labor to each firm is again perfectly elastic. Thus, the supply of labor to the firm in Figure 7.5 (b) becomes S*, and MFC* is $124.00. As a consequence of the decrease in MFC, potential profits have materialized, illustrated by the hatched area in Figure 7.5 (b). Because this firm is assumed to maximize profits, it will increase its employment of labor from five workers to six workers. Thus, *if* the wage rate were to decrease to $124.00, *then* the firm would choose to change its employment in the opposite direction, to increase its employment from five to six workers.

If the firm is purely competitive in its labor market, what schedule solves for the quantity demanded of labor at various alternative wages? The schedule of the value of the marginal physical product of labor solves for quantity, given price. Thus, the schedule of the VMPP of labor is the firm's short-run demand for labor in purely competitive (both product and labor) markets.

The Wage Equals VMPP: An Alternative Interpretation   In purely competitive labor markets, the wage that a worker receives tends to equal the VMPP of the last worker employed. Thus, in Figure 7.5 the wage is $124, a wage equal to the VMPP of the last worker employed and the amount by which the firm's total revenue would change from removing any one of the six workers from employment. (Recall that all workers are homogeneous in the purely competitive model.) What is it about the purely competitive model that guarantees that workers tend to receive a wage equal to the maximum amount that profit-maximizing firms are willing to pay?

Recall the two assumptions of the purely competitive model in the labor market. First, there are enough firms so that the actions of any one firm do not affect the market demand for labor and, therefore, the wage rate. From the perspective of an individual worker, this assumption confronts a worker

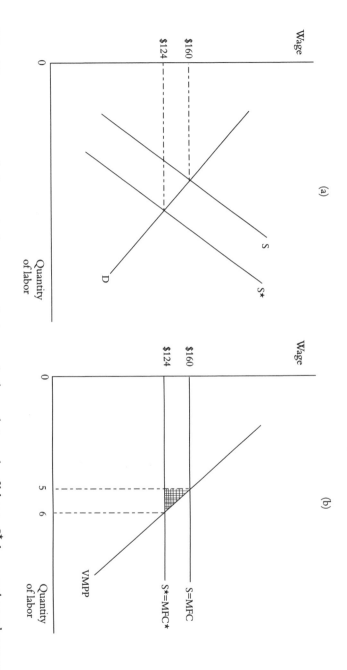

(a)

(b)

Figure 7.5   The consequence of a decrease in the wage rate. An increase in the market supply of labor to S* decreases the market wage to $124, and the supply of labor to the purely competitive firm becomes perfectly elastic at that wage. The firm can now increase its profits (the hatched area) by increasing its employment to six workers.

with the widest possible number of options in employment: all those firms that hire the worker's occupation. Second, the assumption that all firms view workers as homogeneous means there is no reason that any potential employer will exclude a worker because of any personal characteristic such as age, sex, or race. From the perspective of employers, all workers are alike. Given these two assumptions, the supply of labor to each firm in the market is perfectly elastic. What if the firm in Figure 7.5 concluded that it could not afford to pay the wage of $124 and attempted to pay a lower wage – say $115? In purely competitive labor markets, all the workers currently employed with this firm would immediately quit and go to other firms. Thus, it is the wide number of options that workers confront in employment that generates the perfectly elastic supply of labor to each firm in purely competitive labor markets. It is this wide array of options that guarantees that workers receive a wage equal to their contribution to the firm's total revenues.

7.5   THE MARKET DEMAND FOR LABOR

Assume for purposes of illustration that there are only three firms in the market as demanders of labor. Figure 7.6 generates a market demand for labor in this set of circumstances. At a market wage of $160, the first firm employs 5 workers, the second firm hires 12 workers, and the third firm employs 8 workers. The market quantity demanded of labor at $160 is the sum of these quantities employed by the three firms at this wage: 25 workers. When the wage falls to $124, all three firms increase their employment of labor: the first firm to 6 workers, the second firm to 16 workers, and the third firm to 10 workers. Again, the market quantity demanded of labor at $124 is merely the sum of the quantities demanded of labor by the firms in the market at that wage: 32 workers. Thus, the market demand for labor is the sum of the quantities demanded of labor by all the firms in the market at various alternative prices of labor.

7.6   ELASTICITY OF DEMAND FOR LABOR

The firm's demand for labor has a negative slope; if the wage rate were to increase, a profit-maximizing firm would decrease its employment of labor. Elasticity of demand for labor raises a further question: if the wage rate were to increase by, say, 1 percent, how much would the employment of labor decrease? Again, there are only three possibilities: by more than 1 percent, by 1 percent, or by less than 1 percent. If a 1 percent increase in the wage rate led to a decrease of more than 1 percent in the quantity demanded of

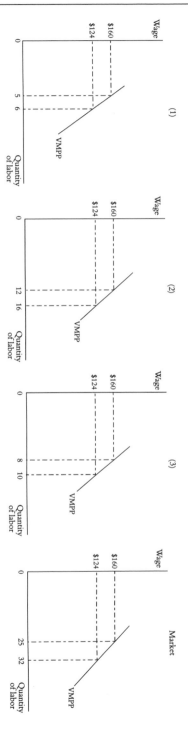

Figure 7.6   The market demand for labor. If the wage rate were $160, then the quantity demanded of labor by all the firms in this market would be 25. If the wage were to fall to $124, then the market quantity demanded of labor would increase to 32. The market demand for labor illustrates the quantity demanded of labor by all firms in a market at various alternative wage rates.

labor, then the demand for labor is elastic. If the 1 percent increase causes the employment of labor to decrease by exactly 1 percent, then the demand for labor is unitarily elastic. If the 1 percent increase in the wage rate causes the quantity demanded of labor to decrease by less than 1 percent, then labor demand is inelastic. Again, there are also the two limit cases. If a 1 percent increase in the wage rate causes zero change in employment, then the demand for labor is perfectly inelastic. If this 1 percent rise leads to an infinitely large decrease in the employment of labor, then the demand for labor is perfectly elastic. This is the standard terminology used before in the discussion of elasticity of product demand. The discussion of the determinants of elasticity of demand for labor, however, necessarily becomes somewhat more complicated.

It is helpful to present the determinants of the elasticity of demand for labor as a series of four propositions. The demand for labor will be more elastic:

1. the more elastic the demand for the product that labor produces.
2. the higher the ratio of labor costs to total costs of production.
3. the easier the substitutability of other inputs for labor.
4. the more elastic the supply of capital.

You have not encountered the phrase "more elastic" before. What does this mean? The demand for labor is elastic if a 1 percent change in the wage leads to a change of more than 1 percent in the employment of labor. For example, if a 1 percent increase in the wage rate leads to a 3 percent decrease in employment, then the demand for labor would be elastic. The demand for labor would also be elastic if that 1 percent increase in the wage led to a 4 percent decrease in employment. The demand for labor would be more elastic, however, in the second case. Because the elasticity of labor demand is defined as the percentage change in the quantity demanded of labor divided by the percentage change in the wage rate, it might be helpful to think "the greater the change in quantity" when you see the phrase "the more elastic."

Elasticity of Demand for the Product   Given the productivity of labor, an increase in the wage rate increases the firm's costs of production. Thus, to a firm, an increase in the wage rate is a disequilibrating event; any profit-maximizing producer will adjust to a rise in the price of an input. However, the adjustment to a rise in the wage rate will not necessarily be in the labor market; the labor market is not the only market in which a firm can adjust to a rise in the price of labor. The firm may be able to adjust by raising the price of its output, simply passing the increase in production costs on to consumers in the form of higher prices. To construct a scenario where this adjustment is impossible, confront the producer with an elastic demand for its product. If the demand for its product is elastic, then a rise in the price of its product (by any percentage amount) will lead to a larger percentage decrease in the sales of its output so that its total revenues fall. No profit-maximizing producer would ever knowingly raise product price if, by doing so, its total revenues would fall.

The degree to which a profit-maximizing firm will adjust in the labor market to a rise in the price of labor depends, in part, on the options for adjustment available to it in the product market. To the degree that adjustments in the product market are ruled out, the firm's adjustment will increasingly be in the labor market. Stated informally, this generalization becomes: the greater the loss in the firm's sales given any increase in the price of its output, the greater will be the resulting loss in its employment of labor given any initial rise in the wage rate. Or, stated formally: the more elastic the demand for the product that labor produces, the more elastic the demand for labor.

The Higher the Ratio of Labor Costs to Total Costs of Production
Assume that wages rise by 10 percent. What is the impact on the firm's costs of production of that rise in the price of an input? The answer depends on the portion of total costs represented by wages. Take two cases for illustration. In one case, wages represent 50 percent of the firm's total costs of producing output. Thus, a 10 percent rise in wages increases this firm's costs of production by 5 percent. In a second case, wages represent 25 percent of a firm's total costs of producing output. In this case, the 10 percent rise in wages raises its costs of producing output by only 2.5 percent. In which of these two cases will the firm's decrease in the employment of labor be greater? In case one, where the impact on total costs is greater. A generalization of this argument then becomes: the greater labor costs are as a percentage of total costs of production, the more elastic will be the firm's demand for labor.

The Substitutability of Other Inputs for Labor
A rise in the wage rate not only raises the price of labor absolutely but also raises the price of labor relative to the prices of other inputs. Any profit-maximizing firm will have an incentive to decrease the employment of the input whose price has risen, replacing that input with relatively lower-priced inputs. How much the employment of labor will fall, however, depends on how readily other inputs can be substituted for labor. If a large number of relatively good substitutes are available to replace labor, then any given rise in the wage rate might lead to a relatively large decline in the employment of labor (that is, a relatively elastic demand for labor). By contrast, a rise in the wages of airline pilots is

not likely to induce much substitution in production by airlines because there are few (if any) substitutes for airline pilots. Thus, this generalization becomes: the more readily other inputs can be substituted for labor in a production process, the more elastic will be the demand for labor.

The Elasticity of Supply of Capital If X and Y are substitutes in production, then an increase in the price of X decreases the quantity demanded of X but increases the demand for its substitute Y. Thus, if the price of labor rises, then the demand for capital (and other substitutes for labor) increases, raising the price of capital. The question then arises: how much will the output of capital increase given a rise in its price? This is the question of the elasticity of supply of capital.

The elasticity of supply of capital is defined as the percentage change in the quantity supplied of capital given any percentage change in the price of capital. Consider two possibilities. In the first case, the rise in the price of capital generates substantial increases in the quantity supplied of capital (that is, a relatively elastic supply of capital). In this case, capital becomes readily available as a substitute for labor, resulting in a relatively large decline in the employment of labor. In another case, however, the increase in the price of capital leads to minimal increases in the output of capital. In this case, little capital becomes available to substitute for labor, resulting in a relatively small decrease in the employment of labor. This generalization stated informally becomes: the degree to which firms will substitute capital (or other inputs) for labor given any rise in the price of labor depends in part on the degree to which the output of capital increases given any increase in the price of capital. Or, stated formally: the more elastic the supply of capital, the more elastic will be the demand for labor.

7.7 LABOR DEMAND SUMMARIZED

In this chapter, we have constructed the theory of producer choice so as to reach a conclusion in the labor market: labor demand. The schedule of the VMPP of labor is the firm's demand for labor because that schedule satisfies the two interpretations that any demand schedule must satisfy. In the first interpretation, the maximum wage that a profit-maximizing firm will pay various workers is the VMPP of the workers. In the second interpretation, the VMPP schedule stipulates what the firm's employment of labor will be given various alternative wages. Furthermore, we saw that in purely competitive labor markets the wage rate tends to equal the VMPP of the last worker hired by the firm. Thus, in purely competitive labor markets, firms pay the maximum wage that they are willing to pay. In addition, because the VMPP of labor has a negative slope, a rise in the wage rate leads firms to reduce the employment of labor, the size of that reduction being dependent on the set of factors that determine the elasticity of demand for labor.

7.8 QUESTIONS

1. The presentation of labor demand in this chapter is developed in a goods-producing context. Consider the informal service sector. What would be the effect of a rise in babysitter wages to $15 per hour? Explain.

2. Much is made of the high wages of sports celebrities. Is it possible that a baseball team's total revenue might rise by several million dollars a year by hiring a player with a .367 batting average? Why?

3. Many people think that competition keeps wages down. In the analysis of this chapter, workers receive the maximum amount that firms are willing to pay (their VMPP) in purely competitive markets. Thus, pure competition keeps wages up. Why the difference in perceptions?

4. How elastic will the demand for unionized airline pilots be? Why?

— 8 —

Labor Supply: A Conclusion of the Theory of Consumer Choice

In Chapter 2, we constructed the theory of consumer choice and reached a conclusion in the product market: product demand. But household members are not only demanders of goods and services; they are also suppliers of labor (and other factor) services. The same theory of consumer choice will generate another conclusion when pursued in the labor market: labor supply. In this chapter, we construct the theory of consumer choice and see that labor supply is a conclusion of that theory.

If the quantity variable in labor supply is measured as worker-hours, then worker-hours can change for two reasons. First, a rise in the wage rate can lead the existing number of workers to work overtime, thus increasing worker-hours. Second, a rise in the wage rate can lead to an increase in the number of workers employed, where all workers work the same average hours as before. Thus, a complete discussion of labor supply requires not only an examination of the number of hours worked but also of the decision to enter or exit the labor force. This second decision is the labor force participation decision. Because the concept of labor force has a precise meaning in economics, it becomes necessary to look into some specifics of labor force data.

The first objective in this chapter is theoretical: to find that labor supply is a conclusion of the theory of consumer choice. Accordingly, a clear conception of labor supply is imperative.

8.1 LABOR SUPPLY DEFINED

Labor supply is a relation between two variables: the wage rate and the quantity supplied of labor. In this relation, the independent variable is the wage rate. Quantity supplied of labor (regardless of how that variable is measured) is the dependent variable. Figure 8.1 illustrates labor supply for an individual. In this illustration, the relation between these two variables is shown to be direct; however, it could also be negative.

Labor supply is subject to two equally valid interpretations. In one interpretation, labor supply is a series of "if, then" statements. Thus, *if* the wage rate in Figure 8.1 were W, *then* this individual would choose to supply the quantity Q hours. *If*, on the other hand, the wage rate were W*, *then* she would increase the quantity supplied of labor to Q* hours.

Labor supply illustrates the minimum wage necessary to induce this individual to supply various quantities of labor hours. Thus, the minimum wage necessary to lead this individual to supply the quantity Q hours is the wage W. A higher wage W* is necessary to induce her to increase the quantity supplied of labor hours to Q*. The immediate objective here is to construct a particular argument: if an individual is assumed to be a utility maximizer, then a change in the wage rate will lead her to change the quantity supplied of labor.

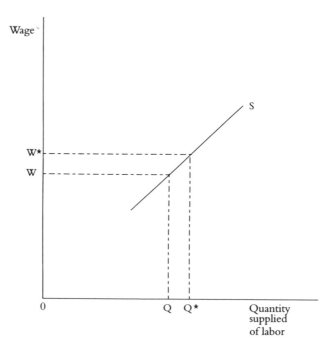

Figure 8.1   The supply of labor. The supply of labor is a relation between the wage rate (the independent variable) and the quantity supplied of labor (the dependent variable).

In product demand, product supply, and labor demand, the expected direction of change of the dependent variable could be deduced. Here it will not be possible to deduce the expected direction of change of the quantity supplied of labor. Thus, the direction of change of the dependent variable ceases to be a theoretical question and becomes instead an empirical (or statistical) question.

8.2 LABOR SUPPLY FOR AN INDIVIDUAL

If an individual is assumed to maximize total utility, then the first step in constructing the theory of consumer choice is to stipulate how total utility varies with the consumption of goods.

Indifference Curves The indifference curves first presented in Chapter 2 illustrated how total utility varied with the quantities consumed of two goods – good X and good Y. Because the objective in that chapter was to derive the individual's demand for good X, that procedure was perfectly satisfactory. Here, however, the objective is to employ the same model of individual choice in order to reach a different conclusion: labor supply. This different objective requires that one define the two goods in such a way that the analysis will yield implications about quantities supplied of labor at various wage rates.

Figure 8.2 illustrates the total utility that an individual receives from consuming various combinations of two goods. The horizontal axis measures quantities of one good – nonmarket time (or leisure time). The vertical axis measures quantities of a composite good – market-produced goods. Combination A contains quantities of each good: X of leisure and Y of market goods. From consuming combination A, the individual receives some level of total utility. Combination B, however, is preferred to combination A because combination B contains no less of one good (Y of market goods) but more of the other good (X^* of leisure rather than X). Combination B, then, lies on a higher indifference curve than does combination A. As before, the slopes of these indifference curves represent the rate at which this individual is willing to make substitutions in consumption, keeping total utility unchanged.

Income Constraints A model of consumer choice is a model of utility maximization subject to constraints. The variable in economic analysis that constrains consumption is real income.

Figure 8.3 illustrates how real income constrains the consumption of both leisure and market goods. Consider leisure. How much leisure could this individual consume if she consumed all of the available time (per week, month, year, or lifetime) as leisure? She could consume the quantity X_M of leisure. But combination P is a combination of two goods. The other quantity in that combination is zero market goods. Thus, by consuming all of the available time as leisure, her consumption of market goods would be zero. Similarly, consider combination Q. This combination indicates the maximum quantity of market goods (Y_M) that this individual could consume if she consumed zero hours as leisure and spent all of the available time working instead. Of course, she could also consume any of the other combinations of these two goods that lie on this income constraint.

As before, an income constraint has both a position and a slope. The position of an income constraint illustrates real income, for it encompasses all combinations of the two goods that are attainable to this individual. To illustrate an increase in real income, shift the income constraint to the right, parallel to itself. By doing so, combinations of these two goods that earlier had not been available to this individual now would be.

By contrast, the slope of this income constraint illustrates something quite

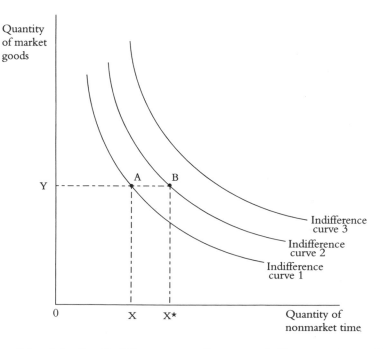

Figure 8.2   A family of indifference curves for two goods. By consuming combination B (X^* nonmarket time and Y market goods) rather than combination A (X nonmarket time and Y market goods), the individual can attain a higher level of total utility.

different. The slope of this income constraint is dY/dX. Notice, however, that given the particular goods Y and X, the slope of this income constraint measures the rate at which leisure can be transformed into market goods. That rate is the wage rate. The slope of the income constraint, therefore, is the wage rate. The wage rate, in turn, is the price of leisure.

One Wage, One Quantity Supplied of Labor   Given the wage rate and given this individual's real income as well as her preferences for market goods and leisure, there is now enough information to decide how much of these two goods she will consume so as to maximize total utility. In Figure 8.4, that combination of two goods is combination A. Combination A contains

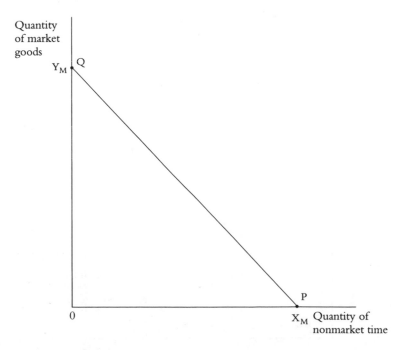

Figure 8.3   An income constraint. If the individual consumed all of the available time as leisure, X_M is the maximum quantity of leisure that could be consumed. Y_M is the maximum quantity of market goods that this individual could consume if none of the available time were time consumed as leisure (and were spent working instead). The attainable combinations of nonmarket time and market goods lie on or within the income constraint. The slope of the income constraint represents the price ratio of the two goods. The rate at which leisure time can be transformed into goods is the wage rate.

Y_A market goods and X_A leisure. Our interest, however, is not in how much leisure this individual will choose to consume, given her preferences, real income, and the price of leisure. Our interest, rather, is in what quantity of labor she will choose to supply at this wage. Can we answer that question based on the information presented in Figure 8.4? Yes, we can. What is the quantity $X_A X_M$? This is the quantity of available time not consumed as leisure. The quantity $X_A X_M$, then, is the quantity supplied of labor at a particular wage (say W, the wage represented by the slope of the income constraint). Thus, you can say that *if* the wage rate is W, *then* this individual will choose to supply the quantity $X_A X_M$ hours of labor. This one combination, however, is not labor supply. Labor supply is a series of "if, then" statements. Thus, you must confront this individual with an alternative wage and raise the question: how would she change the quantity supplied of labor if the wage rose to $W^\star$?

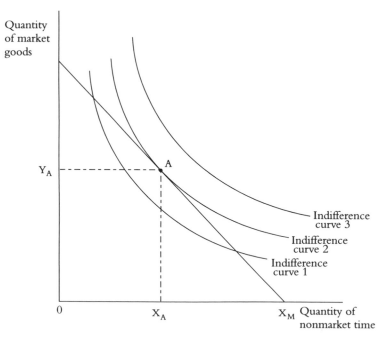

Figure 8.4   One wage, one quantity supplied of labor. Given this individual's preferences, real income, and the price ratios between nonmarket time and market goods, combination A maximizes total utility. Combination A contains X_A nonmarket time. The choice to consume X_A of the available time as leisure is the simultaneous choice not to consume the quantity $X_A X_M$ of the available time as leisure. Thus, $X_A X_M$ is the quantity supplied of labor at this wage.

Reaching the Conclusion Figure 8.5 replicates a portion of Figure 8.4. What is common to each is combination A. Combination A contains X_A of leisure and Y_A of market goods. What you wish to illustrate in Figure 8.5 is how this individual with these preferences changes her behavior in response to a rise in the wage at which she can work.

The wage rate is the rate at which leisure can be transformed into market goods. The slope of the income constraint illustrates this rate. Figure 8.5 illustrates a rise in the wage rate by pivoting the income constraint upward from the horizontal axis. Combinations of these two goods that earlier had not been attainable now are attainable, and from that expanded opportunity set this individual chooses combination B, that attainable combination that yields the highest level of total utility. This combination contains a smaller quantity of leisure $- X_B$. Thus, as a result of the rise in the wage rate (to $W^\star$), this individual chooses to consume less leisure or, rather, to increase the

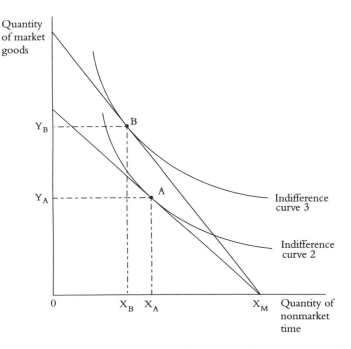

Figure 8.5 A rise in the wage rate. As a result of a rise in the wage rate, combination B becomes the best combination. At combination B this individual consumes less of the available time as leisure (X_B instead of X_A). Thus, a rise in the wage rate results in this individual increasing the quantity supplied of labor by the amount $X_B X_A$.

quantity supplied of labor. These two combinations would, when transferred to a labor supply schedule, trace out the two combinations in Figure 8.1.

In this example, the relation between changes in the wage rate and changes in the quantity supplied of labor by this individual is direct. The relation, however, could just as well have been negative. For reasons that you now encounter, the logical relation between these two variables is theoretically indeterminate.

The Relative Price Effect of a Rise in the Wage Rate   The rise in the wage rate in Figure 8.5 has two separate effects. First, we can see by the change in the slope of the budget constraint that the relative prices of the two goods have changed. But the rise in the wage rate has also enabled this individual to attain a higher level of total utility – combination B is on a higher indifference curve than combination A. Thus, the rise in the wage rate has increased real income as well. As we disentangle the relative price effect (of the wage change) from the income effect (of the wage change), we will understand why the direction of change of the quantity supplied of labor is theoretically indeterminate in labor supply.

Figure 8.6 illustrates both the relative price and income effects of a rise in the wage rate. Consider first the relative price effect alone. What change in the consumption of leisure (and, thus, in the quantity supplied of labor) is due solely to the fact that the price of leisure has risen relative to the price of market goods? Keep the individual's real income unchanged by keeping her on the same indifference curve 2. Then confront her with the new higher price of leisure illustrated by the dashed income constraint. Her new best combination of the two goods is combination C. Combination C contains less leisure–X_C rather than X_A. Thus, the relative price effect of this rise in the wage rate would have, acting alone, decreased the consumption of leisure (increased the quantity supplied of labor) by the amount $X_C X_A$.

The Income Effect of a Rise in the Wage Rate   But a rise in the wage rate also increases real income. Observe in Figure 8.6 that combination B is on a higher indifference curve than combination A. Total utility varies directly with the consumption of goods, and the consumption of goods is constrained by real income. Thus, for an individual to attain a higher level of total utility, real income must have increased. To illustrate an increase in real income, keeping relative prices constant, shift the income constraint to the right, parallel to itself. As you do that, you shift the dashed budget constraint to the right until it is tangent with indifference curve 3 at combination B. Combination B contains X_B of leisure. Thus, the independent effect of an increase in real income leads this individual to increase her consumption of leisure (reduce the quantity supplied of labor) by the amount $X_C X_B$. Thus, to this individual, leisure is a normal good.

The Net Effect of a Rise in the Wage Rate In product demand, a fall in the price of X increases the quantity demanded of X for two reasons: the consumer buys more X as its price falls because X is now cheaper relative to its substitutes; the individual has more real income and increases the consumption of X (if X is a normal good). Thus, the income effect reinforces the relative price effect when X is a normal good. In labor supply, however, the income effect works in opposition to the relative price effect when leisure is a normal good.

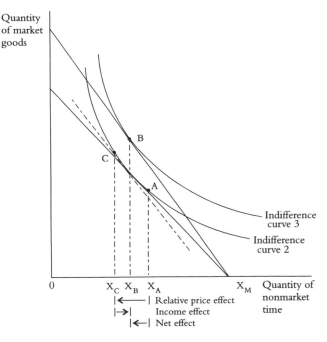

Figure 8.6 Relative price and income effects of a rise in the wage rate. The pure relative price effect of the rise in the wage rate results in this individual's decreasing her consumption of nonmarket time (increasing the quantity supplied of labor) by the quantity $X_C X_A$. The pure income effect of the change in the wage rate results in this individual's increasing the consumption of nonmarket time (decreasing the quantity supplied of labor) by the quantity $X_C X_B$. The net effect of the rise in the wage rate is to decrease the consumption of nonmarket time (increase the quantity supplied of labor) by the amount $X_B X_A$.

Operating alone, the relative price effect says: buy less leisure as its price rises. This is the law of demand with reference to leisure. If the relative price effect were the only effect, then a rise in the wage rate would always lead an individual to reduce the consumption of leisure (increase the quantity supplied of labor). But the rise in the wage also raises real income, and an individual will increase consumption of all normal goods as real income rises. If leisure is a normal good, the increase in real income, operating alone, will increase the consumption of leisure (decrease the quantity supplied of labor).

We cannot deduce which of the two opposing effects will dominate. Thus, economists cannot conclude whether a rise in the wage rate will lead an individual to increase or decrease the quantity supplied of labor. Because the direction of change of the dependent variable cannot be predicted, labor supply is theoretically indeterminant.

The discussion until now has presumed that an individual is already in the labor force. Because such an individual adjusts the hours of labor that she chooses to supply as the wage rate changes, a change in the wage rate does lead to a change in worker-hours in the labor market. But there is a second possible effect as well: the change in the wage rate can induce some other individual who up until now had not been in the labor force to enter the labor force and work a standard workweek. In this case, worker-hours in the labor market would also change, but that change would be due to a change in the number of workers in the market. Any discussion that examines why individuals enter or exit the labor force is a discussion of labor force participation.

8.3   LABOR FORCE PARTICIPATION

This section examines why a change in the wage rate might lead an individual to change her labor force participation. Because the labor force has a precise meaning in economics, some technical considerations are required first.

The Labor Force   The age-eligible population (P) in the United States consists of all noninstitutionalized individuals, 16 years of age or older. As Figure 8.7 indicates, this age-eligible population is in one of two places: in the labor force (L) or not in the labor force. The aggregate labor force participation rate (L/P) is the number of individuals in the labor force (L) as a percentage of the age-eligible population (P).

The labor force is defined as the sum of all those noninstitutionalized individuals, 16 years of age or older (including the military) who are employed (E) or who are unemployed (U). Once each month the Bureau of Labor

Statistics publishes its estimates of the number of employed and unemployed. These estimates are produced from a monthly survey of about 50,000 households. Questions designed to determine the labor force status of household members are asked to each individual (16 years of age or older) in the household. These questions are always asked about the person's activity during the survey week – the week prior to the week in which the survey is administered. What should a person have been doing during the survey week to be classified as employed?

(1) Not surprisingly, a person is classified as employed if she did any work for pay during the survey week. (2) It is, however, also possible that a person can be classified as employed if she worked during the survey week but received no pay. If she worked at least 15 hours in a family-operated enterprise or farm but received no pay, she is employed. (3) It is also possible to classify an individual as employed even though she did no work during the survey week. This would be the case if she was "with a job, not at work." So, for example, if she had a job from which she was temporarily absent during the

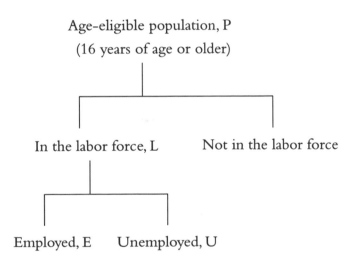

Figure 8.7   The age-eligible population (P) is either in the labor force (L) or not in the labor force. The labor force consists of the sum of it two components: the employed (E) and the unemployed (U). The labor force participation rate is (L/P).

survey week because of vacation, ill health, or bad weather, she would nonetheless be classified as employed even though she did no work during the survey week. A person may be classified as employed, then, if she satisfies criterion (1) or (2) or (3).

A person may be classified as unemployed if (1) she did no work during the survey week. But there has to be more than just this one criterion; otherwise it would be impossible to distinguish this person from the employed person who did no work because she was on vacation. There are indeed two other criteria that the unemployed worker must also meet. (2) The person must be available for work. Thus, if she did no work in March but is not available for work until June, she is not unemployed in March. (3) The individual must have engaged in some specific job-seeking activity during the prior four weeks. Any activity such as registering with an employment service or answering job ads from the newspaper will satisfy this requirement. Thus, for an individual to be classified as unemployed, she must satisfy (l) plus (2) plus (3).

If an individual is classified as neither employed nor unemployed on the basis of activity during the survey week, then that person is not in the labor force. In the aggregate United States economy, a little more than 60 percent of the age-eligible population is in the labor force. Thus, nearly 40 percent of the age-eligible population is not in the labor force.

It is important to realize that individuals are classified as being either in or out of the labor force solely on the basis of their activity during the survey week, not on any other criteria. Thus, an individual's occupation is not sufficient to indicate whether or not she is in the labor force. Some students are in the labor force, others are not. Furthermore, some students are in the labor force for some months of the year, but not others. The same observation holds for homemakers. Some homemakers are employed full-time, some hold dual jobs, some work part-time, and some are not in the labor force and have not been in the labor force since they married.

The Effect of a Rise in the Wage Rate on Labor Force Participation

Given an individual's tastes and preferences and the wage at which she can work, the utility-maximizing quantity of market work may be zero hours. However, a higher wage could induce an individual to enter the labor force. Given the value of a person's activities in nonmarket activities, a rise in the wage rate increases the cost of time spent in those activities and, at the margin, attracts into the labor force those individuals for whom the cost of nonmarket activities now exceeds, at the higher wage, the value they assign to those activities.

Not only does an individual enter the labor force to take a job, she may also enter the labor force to look for a job. In this case, the person's behavior is influenced by the expected wage – the wage offered for individuals in her occupation adjusted by the probability of finding a job that pays that wage. Because job vacancies increase in expansions and fall in contractions, the expected wage is critically sensitive. Economic theory suggests that L/P should also be cyclically sensitive, and the evidence on this point is consistent: the aggregate labor force participation rate (L/P) does rise in periods of economic expansion and fall in periods of contraction.

8.4 THE MARKET SUPPLY OF LABOR

Figure 8.8 illustrates the market supply of labor in a market with three individuals. It also illustrates the variety of experiences that are possible as the wage rate rises from W to W* in this market. As the wage rises, individual 1 increases the quantity supplied of labor from 40 to 42 hours, demonstrating the dominance of the substitution effect. Individual 2 decreases the quantity supplied of labor from 40 to 38 hours, illustrating the dominance of the income effect. Individual 3 is not a labor force participant at wage W but chooses to enter the labor force at wage W* to supply 40 hours. The market supply of labor, S, in Figure 8.8, is the summation of the quantities of labor supplied by the individuals in this market at various alternative wage rates.

8.5 THE ELASTICITY OF SUPPLY OF LABOR

Like any other elasticity measure, elasticity of labor supply measures the percentage change in the dependent variable (quantity supplied of labor) in response to a percentage change in the independent variable (wage rate). As before, a 1 percent change in the wage rate can lead to only three possibilities in the dependent variable. The quantity supplied of labor can change (ignoring in this discussion the direction of the change) by more than 1 percent. In this case, supply is elastic. (At the limit, supply may be perfectly elastic if the change in the dependent variable becomes infinitely large.) The 1 percent change can lead to a change in the quantity supplied of labor of exactly 1 percent. In this case, supply is unitarily elastic. The third possibility is that the 1 percent change leads to a change in the quantity supplied of labor of less than 1 percent. In this case, supply is inelastic. (Again, the limit case here is perfectly inelastic. Labor supply is perfectly inelastic if the change in the wage rate leads to zero change in the quantity supplied of labor.) The question then becomes: what factors determine whether a change in the

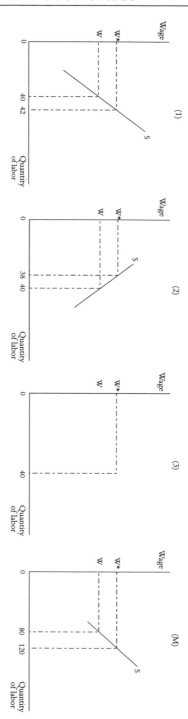

Figure 8.8   The market supply of labor. At wage W, the quantity supplied of labor by all individuals in this market is 80 hours. At the higher wage W* the market quantity supplied increases to 120 hours. The first individual increases hours supplied to 42 hours (a dominant substitution effect), the second individual decreases hours supplied to 38 hours (a dominant income effect), and the third individual, who had not been a labor force participant at the lower wage, enters the labor market to supply 40 hours. The market supply of labor sums the quantities supplied of labor at various alternative wages by all individuals in the market.

market wage will lead to a relatively large or a relatively small change in the quantity supplied of labor?

If the wage W is the market wage for occupation A, then one determinant of the elasticity of the supply of labor to that occupation is the degree to which the skills required in occupation B and other occupations can be transferred into occupation A. The more readily those skills can be transferred into occupation A (or the lower the costs of doing so), the more elastic will be the supply of labor to occupation A.

Time for adjustment is, as always, a determinant of elasticity of supply. The longer one allows for adjustment to take place, the more adjustment there will be. Thus, the longer the time allowed for adjustment, the more elastic the supply of labor.

Most fundamentally, a rise in the wage rate may lead an individual to consume less leisure and work longer hours. Thus, the degree to which that substitution takes place given any change in the wage rate depends, in part, on a subjective characteristic of the individual: the rate at which she is willing to make substitutions in consumption between leisure and market goods. This subjective characteristic will differ across the population.

8.6 LABOR SUPPLY AND THE DISTRIBUTION OF INCOME ACROSS HOUSEHOLDS

There is no formal discussion of the distribution of income across households in this text. This is a large topic that is, itself, the subject of much scholarly effort. Nonetheless, it is appropriate to recognize some implications of this topic when they are relevant. Labor supply presents such an opportunity.

Annual money income is the sum of nonlabor income and labor income. Labor income (Y) is the product of the wage (W) at which a person can work multiplied by the hours (H) that a person chooses to work at that wage: $Y = (W)(H)$. Annual money income across households can differ for a wide number of reasons. For example, different households receive different amounts of nonlabor income; households differ in the number of individuals who are in the age-eligible population; household members differ in the market wage they can earn in their occupation. The discussion in this chapter has led to an appreciation of one other reason. Because household members are assumed to be utility maximizers – not income maximizers – they will differ in the quantity supplied of labor (measured as annual hours) at the market wage for their occupation. Part of this difference may be involuntary; household members do experience unemployment. But individuals who experience no unemployment will still vary in the annual hours they choose to supply. Because individuals differ in the annual quantities of hours they choose to supply at market wages, and because annual hours worked is one determinant of the distribution of annual incomes across households, some portion of the difference in annual incomes across households is chosen.

8.7 QUESTIONS

1. How might tax policies in a nation affect the decision to work overtime?

2. In periods of economic expansion, were all individuals who fill the new job vacancies previously unemployed? What are the implications of your answer for the labor force participation rate?

3. What nonmarket production takes place among individuals who are not in the labor force?

4. For most (if not all) immigrant groups in the United States, annual income is higher than for natives with the same level of education. This is probably because immigrants earn higher wages for given skills than do natives. Comment.

9

A Model of Equilibrium Wage Determination

In labor demand, we assume various alternative wages; the quantity demanded of labor is the dependent variable. In labor supply, we also assume various alternative wages; the quantity supplied of labor is the dependent variable. In this chapter, we no longer assume various alternative wages; rather, we examine those market forces that determine an equilibrium wage and identify those variables that lead to changes in the equilibrium wage rate. As before, the concept of equilibrium is that of no net tendency to change. Thus, an equilibrium wage is a wage that exhibits no net tendency to change.

9.1 EQUILIBRIUM WAGE DETERMINATION

Figure 9.1 presents the market demand (D) for occupation A and the market supply of labor (S) to that same occupation. Assume that the market wage for this occupation were W^*. Would that wage be an equilibrium wage, or would there be a net tendency for W^* to change?

At wage W^*, the market quantity demanded of labor is Q_D. The market quantity supplied of labor at that wage, however, is Q_S. Thus, at wage W^* there is a surplus (or excess supply) of labor. This surplus of labor is referred to as unemployment in the labor market. Given a surplus of labor at wage W^*, there is a net tendency for that wage to fall.

Two adjustments begin to occur as the wage begins to fall below W^*. First, at the lower wage, firms increase the employment of labor. Second, at the lower wage household members reduce the quantity supplied of labor. Both of these adjustments tend to narrow the surplus. The surplus is completely eliminated at wage W_E, where the market quantity demanded of labor (Q_E) is

119

equal to the market quantity supplied of labor (Q_E) at that wage. Because there exist no further tendencies for this wage to fall, W_E is an equilibrium wage rate. It is the downward adjustment in the market wage that is the equilibrating mechanism in this market, because it is the downward adjustment in the wage that brings the market quantity demanded of labor into equality with the quantity supplied of labor.

Assume, by contrast, that the wage were below its equilibrium value, such as wage W^* in Figure 9.2. At wage W^*, the market quantity demanded of labor by firms (Q_D) exceeds the market quantity supplied of labor by household members (Q_S). Thus, at that wage there is a shortage of (or excess demand for) labor. A shortage of labor leads to a rise in the market wage. As the wage begins to rise, two adjustments take place: firms reduce their employment of labor as the wage rises; household members increase the quantity of labor they supply at higher wages. The wage rate continues to rise until the shortage has

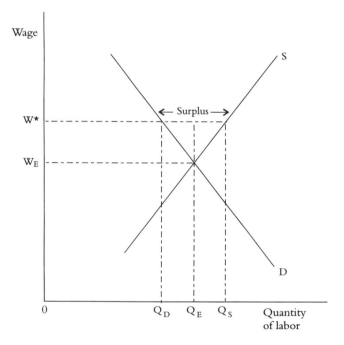

Figure 9.1   A surplus of labor at wage W^*. Given the market demand for labor and the market supply of labor, a surplus of labor would exist at W^*. The existence of a surplus puts downward pressure on the wage rate. As the wage falls, firms increase the employment of labor; labor suppliers decrease the quantity supplied of labor. W_E is an equilibrium wage, a wage that exhibits no net tendency to change. At that wage, the equilibrium quantity employed of labor is Q_E.

been eliminated. At W_E, there is no shortage because the market quantity demanded of labor at that wage exactly equals the market quantity supplied of labor at that wage. W_E, then, is an equilibrium wage rate.

9.2   WAGE FLOORS: MINIMUM-WAGE LEGISLATION

The Fair Labor Standards Act of 1938 established a legal minimum wage in the United States and specified the sectors of the economy in which employers are legally obligated by the provisions of the law to pay at least the minimum wage. Over time, that legislation has been amended in two directions: both the legal minimum itself and the sectors of the economy in which employers are covered by the provisions of the law have been steadily increased. The overwhelming percentage of individuals in the labor force are presently in sectors of the economy covered by the provisions of the minimum-wage law.

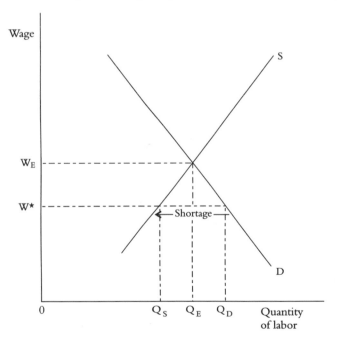

Figure 9.2   A shortage of labor at wage $W^\star$. Given the market demand for labor and the market supply of labor, a shortage of labor would exist at $W^\star$. The existence of a shortage puts upward pressure on the wage rate. As the wage rises, firms decrease their employment of labor; labor suppliers increase the quantity supplied of labor. W_E is an equilibrium wage, a wage that exhibits no net tendency to change. At that wage, Q_E is the equilibrium volume of employment.

For a minimum-wage law to have an adverse impact on employment, it must exceed the market wage for that category of labor. The adverse employment effects of a minimum wage can be examined by referring again to Figure 9.1. Let W^* be the minimum wage. Let W_E be the market wage in the absence of the legislation. Thus, wage W^* is a supported price, supported in this case by federal legislation. The effect on employment is straightforward: less labor is employed at W^* than at W_E.

Who will lose jobs at a minimum wage of \$4.50? For example, will the employment loss be scattered equally across occupations and industries or will it be concentrated? Economic theory predicts that the employment loss will be concentrated among those workers with VMPPs at or around \$4.50. The employment of higher-skilled, higher-productivity workers will be largely (if not totally) unaffected by the minimum wage. Thus, the employment loss will be concentrated among the lowest-skilled members of the labor force. Individuals with the lowest levels of education and work experience are in this group. This group will also include teenagers, who generally have low levels of work experience.

Although the lowest skilled workers and teenagers bear the brunt of the employment loss due to the minimum wage, workers in some minority groups are especially impacted. There is an excess supply of workers at W^*; in Figure 9.1 employers are required to ration the available jobs (Q_D) among a larger quantity of job seekers (Q_S) using some nonwage rationing mechanism. Social connections are always of some consequence in the world, but in labor markets with minimum-wage laws, social connections take on an even larger importance because employers will be inclined to offer jobs to workers they know (or whose parents they know). Studies of workers actually employed at the minimum wage indicate that a disproportionate number are younger workers from middle- and upper-income households.

Why would elected representatives in a democratic society choose to enact minimum-wage legislation when that legislation imposes such costs on the least advantaged groups in society? The answer is because some groups in society benefit from minimum-wage legislation. A complete investigation of who those beneficiaries are and on what grounds politicians would choose to support or oppose minimum-wage legislation is a discussion that properly belongs to the area of public-choice economics.

9.3   CHANGES IN THE MARKET DEMAND FOR LABOR

If the equilibrium wage rate is determined by the interaction of the market demand for labor and the market supply of labor, then any factor that causes either of these determinants to change will lead to changes in the equilibrium wage. Consider changes in the market demand for labor.

Increases in the Market Demand for Labor Figure 9.3 illustrates an increase in the market demand for labor from D to D*. Because both schedules can be interpreted as a series of "if, then" statements, how does D* differ from D? It used to be the case that *if* the wage were W, *then* the market quantity demanded at that wage would be Q. Now the market quantity demanded at that wage is larger–Q*. Furthermore, there is nothing unique about this combination. The same statement can be made about the quantities at each wage. Thus, an increase in the market demand for labor increases the market quantity demanded of labor at every wage.

The demand for labor has a second equally valid interpretation. That schedule indicates the maximum wage the firm is willing to pay various

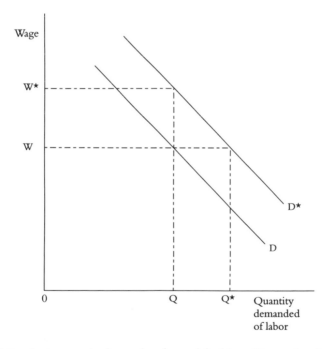

Figure 9.3　An increase in the market demand for labor. The market demand for labor increases from D to D*. Whereas the quantity demanded of labor at wage W had been Q in this market, that quantity has now increased to Q*. Alternatively, whereas the maximum wage that employers in this market had been willing to pay Q workers had been W, now that maximum wage for this quantity has increased to W*.

quantities of labor. Earlier, the maximum wage that the firms were willing to pay the quantity Q was W. Now that maximum wage is higher (W*) for that quantity. Firms are now willing to pay a higher wage than before for all quantities of labor. Thus, an increase in the market demand for labor increases the maximum wage that firms are willing to pay for every quantity of labor.

Decreases in the Market Demand for Labor   Figure 9.4 illustrates a decrease in the market demand for labor. Earlier, the market quantity demanded of labor at wage W was Q. Now, because of the decline in the market demand for labor to D*, the market quantity demanded of labor at wage W is less–Q*. Thus, a decrease in the market demand for labor decreases the market quantity demanded of labor at every wage.

Alternatively, a decrease in the market demand for labor decreases the maximum wage that firms are willing to pay various quantities of labor. Given market demand D, the maximum wage that firms were willing to pay Q

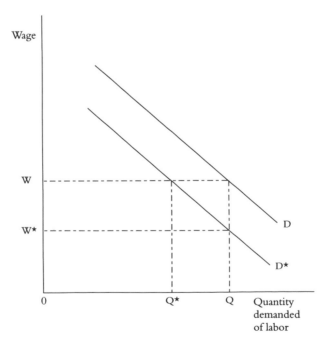

Figure 9.4   A decrease in the market demand for labor. The market demand for labor decreases from D to D*. Whereas the quantity demanded of labor at W had been Q in this market, now that quantity has decreased to Q*. Alternatively, the maximum wage that employers in this market are willing to pay Q workers has decreased from W to W*.

workers was W. Now, because of the decrease in the market demand to D^*, that maximum wage is now lower—W^*.

What factors cause the market demand for labor to increase?

Increases in the MPP of Labor   The demand for labor is a schedule of the VMPP of labor. The VMPP of labor is the product of two variables: the marginal physical product of labor (MPP) multiplied by marginal revenue (MR). Thus, any factor that causes the MPP of labor to increase will increase the market demand for labor.

Table 7.1 (page 92) presented some hypothetical data on the MPP of workers employed in the production of brooms in the short run. In that table, the fifth worker added 80 brooms to output. Why was that output 80 brooms and not 120 brooms? To generate the MPP of labor in Table 7.1, hold the employment of capital constant ($K^* = 3$). To that fixed amount of capital add successive amounts of the variable input labor. The particular schedule of the MPP of labor in the table is the result of the particular quantities of capital and labor employed in this production process. This schedule is represented as MPP' in Figure 9.5. What if, by contrast, the employment of capital had been five units ($K^* = 5$)? If successive amounts of labor are employed with a larger (but still fixed) amount of capital, then the MPP of each input of labor increases. This is schedule MPP^* in Figure 9.5. Thus, one variable that increases the schedule of the MPP of labor is an increase in the capital (and other resources) with which labor works. A worker employed with a combine harvester generates greater output per worker-hour than the same worker employed with a hoe.

As illustrated in Figure 9.6, an increase in the market demand for labor due to an increase in the MPP of labor has further effects: it leads to changes in the equilibrium wage and employment of labor. The increase in the market demand for labor to D^* creates an excess demand for (or a shortage of) labor at wage W_E. Excess demand leads to a rise in the equilibrium wage to W_E^* and an increase in the equilibrium employment of labor to Q_E^*. Thus, an increase in the capital intensity of production (that is, the amount of capital and other inputs used with labor in production) increases the demand for labor and increases both the equilibrium wage and volume of employment.

This logical result will seem counterintuitive to those who imagine that capital displaces labor in production. But the greater amounts of capital relative to labor employed in production increase the MPP of labor and thus the VMPP of labor, the maximum amount that firms are willing to pay labor. Because VMPP is the firm's demand for labor, increases in the MPP of labor increase the demand for labor.

Improvements in Technology   The MPP schedule illustrates output per unit input of labor, given technology. Thus, an improvement in technology, given the inputs of capital and labor in the production process, will increase the schedule of the MPP of labor (MPP* instead of MPP' in Figure 9.5). Because improvements in technology are often embedded in particular forms of capital, it is sometimes difficult to disentangle output changes due to improvements in technology from output changes resulting from increases in the quantities of capital (and other factors) employed in production. Nonetheless, those are difficulties of measurement that can be ignored for these purposes. The independent effects of improvements in technology are clear: they increase the MPP of labor and thus increase the demand for labor. Because improvements in technology increase the market demand for labor, they increase both the equilibrium wage and employment of labor.

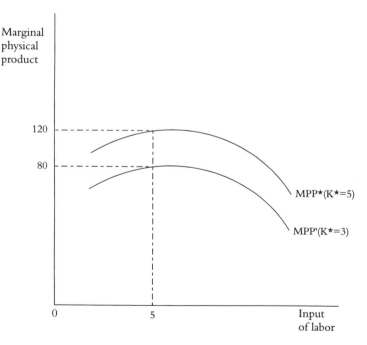

Figure 9.5   Increases in the marginal physical product of labor. An increase in capital employed in a production process increases the productivity of labor employed there. Thus, by increasing the employment of capital from 3 units to 5 units, the output attained by employing the fifth worker increases from 80 units to 120 units.

An Increase in the Demand for the Product   The demand for all factors of production is a derived demand. This means that the demand for labor is not a final demand but is derived from a final demand. That final demand is consumers' demand for output. Thus, any increase in the demand for output should increase the demand for labor used to produce the output. How exactly does an increase in the demand for grapes increase the demand for grapepickers?

The demand for grapepickers is a schedule of the VMPP of grapepickers. The VMPP of grapepickers is a product of two variables: (MPP) × (MR). For an increase in the demand for grapes to increase the VMPP of grapepickers, it must increase either the MPP of grapepickers or the firm's MR (the addition to the firm's total revenues from selling the grapes). First note that there is no connection between increases in the demand for grapes and the MPP of

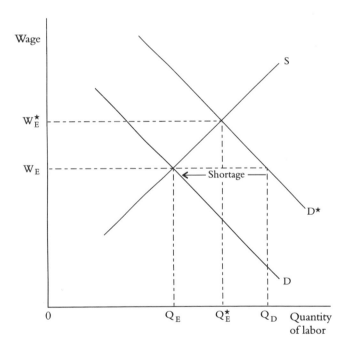

Figure 9.6   The effect of productivity gains on wages and employment. An increase in the productivity of labor increases the demand for labor from D to D★. The shortage of labor at W_E that this increase in demand creates is eliminated by the upward movement of the wage to $W_E^\star$. At $W_E^\star$, the equilibrium volume of employment becomes $Q_E^\star$. Thus, improvements in the productivity of labor increase both wages and employment.

grapepickers. There is, however, a clear connection between increases in the demand for grapes and MR. In purely competitive product markets, MR equals product price. An increase in the demand for grapes increases the price of grapes. Thus, an increase in the demand for grapes increases VMPP, that rise coming from the increase in the selling price of grapes. Increases in the market demand for grapepickers increase both the equilibrium wage and employment of grapepickers.

An Increase in the Number of Firms in the Labor Market An increase in the number of firms growing grapes increases the market demand for grapepickers. This variable is analogous to population cited earlier in Chapter 4 as a determinant of the market demand for X. As before, an increase in the market demand for grapepickers will raise both the equilibrium wage and employment of grapepickers.

9.4 CHANGES IN THE MARKET SUPPLY OF LABOR

Changes in the equilibrium wage and volume of employment can also occur because of changes in the market supply of labor.

An Increase in the Market Supply of Labor Figure 9.7 illustrates an increase in the market supply of labor from S to S*. Originally, the market quantity supplied of labor at wage W was Q. Now, the market quantity supplied of labor at that wage is Q*. Thus, an increase in the market supply means that the market quantity supplied of labor at every wage is now greater than it was.

It is also correct to say that an increase in the market supply of labor reduces the minimum wage at which various quantities of labor are willing to work. Thus, the minimum wage at which the quantity Q is willing to work was initially W. Now Q workers are willing to work at the lower wage W*.

A Decrease in the Market Supply of Labor Figure 9.8 illustrates a decrease in the market supply of labor from S to S*. Originally, the market quantity supplied of labor at wage W was Q. Now, because of the decrease in the market supply of labor, the market quantity supplied of labor at that wage is less – Q*. Thus, a decrease in the market supply of labor can be interpreted as a decrease in the market quantity supplied of labor at every wage.

Alternatively, a decrease in the market supply of labor increases the minimum wage at which various quantities of labor are available for work. Earlier, the minimum wage that Q workers were willing to accept was W. Now the minimum wage for that quantity is higher – W*.

The Effects of Increases in the Market Supply of Labor Figure 9.9 illustrates the effects of an increase in the market supply of labor on both the equilibrium wage and employment of labor. The first effect is an excess supply of labor at wage W_E. There will be downward pressures on the market wage resulting from this excess supply, the new equilibrium wage falling to W_E^*. But the volume of employment expands to Q_E^*. Thus, given sufficient time, any labor market can adjust to an increase in the supply of labor with no permanent unemployment so long as the wage is flexible downward. This adjustment is not easy, however, and workers in an occupation frequently resist the entry of new workers.

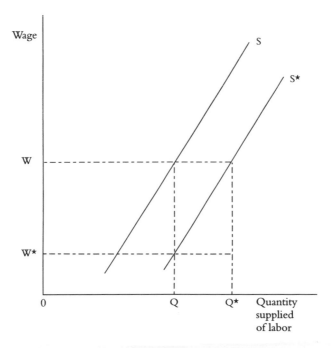

Figure 9.7   An increase in the market supply of labor. The market supply of labor increases from S to S*. Whereas the quantity supplied of labor at W had been Q in this market, that quantity has now increased to Q*. Alternatively, whereas the minimum wage that labor suppliers were willing to accept to supply Q hours of labor had been W, that minimum wage has now decreased to W*.

9.5 QUESTIONS

1. Organized labor lobbies Congress to raise the minimum wage. But individuals who earn wages at or around the minimum wage tend not to belong to unions. Might unions nonetheless benefit from legislation that raises the wages of workers who are not members of unions?

2. Deregulation of the airlines has resulted in substantial declines in airline fares. What are the predictable consequences in the labor market of airline deregulation?

3. There is evidence to show that the greater the productivity gains in an industry, the greater is the employment growth in that industry. Can this evidence be understood from the analysis in this chapter? Explain.

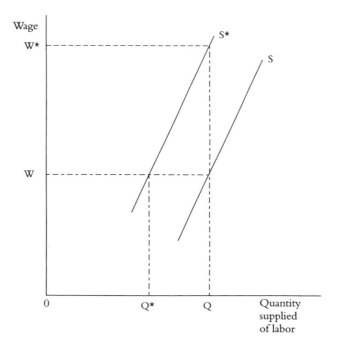

Figure 9.8 A decrease in the market supply of labor. The market supply of labor decreases from S to S*. Whereas the quantity supplied of labor at W had been Q in this market, that quantity has now decreased to Q*. Alternatively, whereas the minimum wage that labor suppliers were willing to accept to supply Q hours had been W, that minimum wage has now increased to W*.

4. The migration of more than half a million Cuban immigrants into south Florida in recent decades can be understood with reference to Figure 9.7. (Economists sometimes refer to an increase in quantities of migrants at given wages as exogenous migration.) Is it your understanding that this huge influx of migrants into south Florida has resulted in permanently low wages and high unemployment there? Explain.

5. Although the development agency in a state may actively recruit new industry, existing firms in the state will often oppose the entry of new producers. Why?

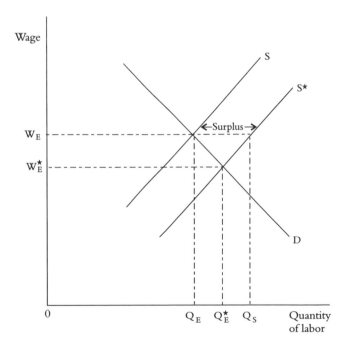

Figure 9.9 The effects of an increase in the market supply of labor. The market supply of labor increases from S to S*. This increase in market supply creates a surplus of labor at W_E that is eliminated by the decrease in the equilibrium wage to W_E^*. At this new equilibrium wage, the equilibrium volume of employment becomes Q_E^*.

——— 10 ———

Long-Run Tendencies in Purely Competitive Labor Markets

Given the annual hours that you work, increases in the wage at which you can work increase your annual income. Given your skills, can you earn a higher wage by employing those skills in another industry or region? In this chapter, we discover that average real wages for like types of labor tend toward equality across both industries and regions in purely competitive labor markets. Thus, in purely competitive labor markets, individuals cannot on average earn higher real wages by employing their given skills in other industries or regions. This chapter identifies those features of purely competitive labor markets that generate this very powerful tendency toward equality of wages for like types of labor.

10.1 AVERAGE REAL WAGES FOR OCCUPATION A: EQUALITY ACROSS INDUSTRIES

The conclusion that we reach in this section is very precise: the average real wage for like types of labor tends toward equality across industries in purely competitive labor markets. First, the wage is an average wage. In any labor market, there will be a distribution of actual wages around a mean. Although economic theory can explain the distribution of actual wages around a mean, the interest here is the mean, not the distribution around the mean. Second, the average wage is an average real wage. A real wage is the purchasing power of the money wage. Third, the wage is an average real wage for like types of labor. This final stipulation requires a more substantial discussion.

To begin with, there is no proposition in economic theory to suggest that all workers will tend to receive the same average real wage. Workers differ in

133

their productivity-related characteristics, such as years of education and work experience, and those differences generate differences in average real wages across workers. Characteristics of occupations other than wages differ as well, and these differences also generate differences in average real wages across workers. So, for example, economic theory does not conclude that the average real wage for electricians will tend toward the average real wage for physicians. Economic theory does conclude, however, that the average real wage for electricians will tend toward equality across industries. Thus, electricians employed in the clothing industry will tend to earn the same average real wage as electricians in the auto industry.

Finally, concluding that the average real wage for like types of labor tends toward equality across industries is not the same as concluding that the average real wage tends toward equality across industries. Different industries employ different occupational mixes of workers. Industry A may employ mostly high-wage occupations; industry B, on the other hand, may employ largely low-wage occupations. If one measured the average wage (total wages divided by the number of workers employed) in industry A, that wage would be higher than in industry B. Nonetheless, at the same time that the average wage in industry A is higher than in industry B, it is also the case that for any occupation X there will be no difference in the average real wage between industries A and B.

With these considerations in mind, what analysis leads to the conclusion that the average real wage for like types of labor tends toward equality across industries in purely competitive labor markets?

Wage Differences in the Short Run   Figure 10.1 illustrates the industry demand for occupation A (D_A) and the short-run supply of labor to that occupation (S_A). The resulting equilibrium wage is W_E and the equilibrium quantity of labor employed in this occupation is Q_E. Now let the demand for the industry's output increase. This increase in product demand increases product-selling price, which in purely competitive product markets is MR to the firm. Because MR is one of the determinants of the demand for labor (VMPP), the industry demand for occupation A increases to D_A^*. This increase in the industry demand for occupation A increases the wage in this occupation to W^*. The increase in the market wage also leads to an increase in the quantity of worker-hours employed in occupation A in this industry from Q_E to Q'. This short-run increase in worker-hours employed is due primarily to increases in hours worked by workers in occupation A already employed in the industry. (If the increase in the industry demand for labor from D_A to $D_A^\star$ had been due to an increase in the MPP of workers in that occupation, the effects on wages and employment would have been identical.)

The increase in the industry demand for occupation A (regardless of the source of the increase) does cause the average wage for occupation A in that industry to rise to $W^\star$ in the short run. Thus, in the short run, the average wage in this occupation does rise relative to the average wage for that occupation in some other industry. This difference in the average wage for occupation A across industries is only a short-run phenomenon, however.

Wage Differences in the Long Run   The increase in the average wage of occupation A in this industry increases the attractiveness of this industry to

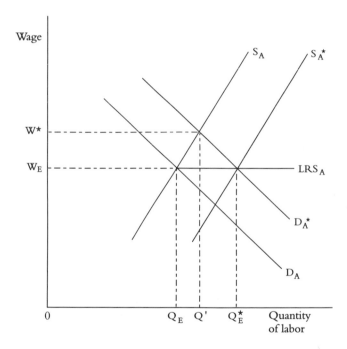

Figure 10.1   Industrial wage differences in the short run and in the long run. An increase in the industry demand for occupation A from D_A to $D_A^\star$ raises the wage of that occupation to $W^\star$ in the short run. At that higher wage, employment of occupation A in this industry increases to Q'. Because the wage for occupation A is now higher in this industry, the supply of labor to this industry increases from S_A to $S_A^\star$. The long-run equilibrium combination of wages and employment becomes W_E and $Q_E^\star$. Thus, the long-run supply of labor in occupation A to this industry is perfectly elastic at W_E.

workers in occupation A. It does take time for information of the higher wage in this industry to spread, and it also takes time for workers employed in occupation A in other industries to act on the new information. The model of pure competition does not include the assumption that information is a free good or that adjustment to change is costless. But the model does include the assumption that there are no barriers to the movement of workers in occupation A across industries. When this adjustment does take place, the short-run supply of labor in occupation A to this industry increases, illustrated by the increase in the short-run supply of labor from S_A to S_A^* in Figure 10.1. This increase in the short-run supply has two effects. First, it reduces the average wage in occupation A in this industry from W^* to W_E. Second, employment of this occupation in this industry increases from Q' to Q_E^*. In the long run, it is the increase in the short-run supply of workers to occupation A that increases employment in this industry and erodes the wage premium that workers in occupation A had been receiving in this industry. Thus, in the long run, the average wage for like types of labor will tend toward equality across industries.

There are two equilibrium combinations illustrated in Figure 10.1. First, given the initial industry demand (D_A) and initial short-run supply (S_A), the wage W_E and the quantity Q_E represent one equilibrium combination. The wage W_E and quantity Q_E^* is a second equilibrium combination. (The combination W^* and Q' is not an equilibrium combination because wage W^* leads to the entry of additional workers into this industry.) Equilibrium combinations contain the minimum wage necessary to induce various quantities of labor in occupation A to this industry. Because no wage premium is necessary to induce various quantities of labor in occupation A to this industry in the long run, the long-run supply of labor in occupation A to this industry (LRS_A) is horizontal (perfectly elastic) at the wage W_E.

The logical conclusion that individuals in purely competitive labor markets cannot, on average, increase the real wage at which they can work (given their skills) by changing industries still leaves open the possibility that they may be able to do so by changing regions. Thus, consider next whether there is any tendency for the average real wage for like types of labor to tend toward equality across regions.

10.2 AVERAGE REAL WAGES FOR OCCUPATION A: EQUALITY ACROSS REGIONS IN A NATION

This discussion continues to refer to an average real wage for like types of labor. It examines, however, whether the average real wage for like types of labor tends toward equality across regions within a nation. Thus, for example, do certified public accountants with identical years of experience tend to earn the same average real wage in the North as they do in the South? Economic theory does predict that average real wages for like types of labor will tend toward equality in purely competitive labor markets. The objective here is to see what adjustment mechanisms bring about this conclusion.

Changes in the Regional Supplies of Labor   Figure 10.2 illustrates a difference in the average wage for occupation A in the North and South. In the North, the demand for occupation A (D_N) and the supply of occupation A (S_N) establish a market wage W_N. In the South, the demand for occupation A (D_S) and the supply of occupation A (S_S) establish a lower wage W_S. Workers employed in occupation A in the South can increase their wage by migrating. As they do so, the supply of labor in the South decreases to $S_S^\star$, increasing the average wage in the South to $W_S^\star$. Conversely, the supply of labor in the receiving region increases to $S_N^\star$, thus decreasing the average wage in the North to $W_N^\star$. The migration of labor, therefore, is one mechanism that acts to narrow the average real wage for like types of labor across regions.

Changes in the Regional Demands for Labor   Changes in the relative demands for labor across regions in a nation will also work to eliminate differences in the average real wage for like types of labor across those regions. For example, if the average wage for occupation A were higher in the North than in the South, how would adjustments on the demand side eliminate that difference?

Figure 10.3 illustrates the demand for occupation A in the North (D_N) and the supply of labor to that occupation in the North (S_N) resulting in the wage W_N in the North. In the South, the demand for labor (D_S) and the supply of labor (S_S) generate a market wage W_S. When you recall that the demand for labor is the schedule of the VMPP of labor, you realize immediately that changes in the demand for labor can occur for two reasons. First, consider a change in the MPP of labor. Profit-maximizing firms in the North observe that the costs of producing output are lower in the South and move *new* plant and equipment into that region. As the South thus imports capital and other productive resources, the MPP of labor increases in the South, increasing the VMPP of labor in the South to $D_S^\star$ and raising the average wage of labor in that region to $W_S^\star$. This adjustment alone is sufficient to narrow the North–South wage difference. But there is a further possible adjustment as well. Some firms in the North may relocate to the South, thus moving existing plant and

Figure 10.2 Changes in the regional supplies of labor. The demand for labor in the North (D_N) and the supply of labor in the North (S_N) establish a market wage W_N in the North. Similarly, the demand for labor in the South (D_S) and the supply of labor in the South (S_S) establish a market wage W_S in the South. The higher wage in the North leads to the migration of some southern workers, decreasing the supply of labor in the South to S_S^* and increasing the supply of labor in the North to S_N^*. These shifts in the supply of labor in each region act to narrow the North–South wage difference.

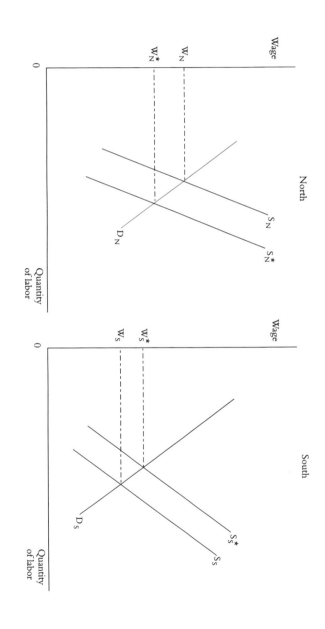

Figure 10.3   Changes in the regional demands for labor. Two possible adjustments in the regional demands for labor will narrow wage differences across regions. If wages are initially higher in the North than in the South, the lower costs of production in the South lead northern producers to locate new capital in the South, increasing the southern demand for labor to D_S^* and raising wages in the South to W_S^*. If northern producers relocate existing capital from the North to the South in response to this difference in costs of production, the demand for labor in the North will decrease to D_N^*, thus further narrowing the wage difference. The change in the regional demand for labor can also occur because of changes in product prices across regions. If lower costs of production in the South lead to lower product prices from southern producers, then consumers will increase their demand for southern output and decrease their demand for northern output. The rise in the price of southern output will increase the demand for labor there to D_S^*. The decrease in the price of northern output will decrease the demand for labor there to D_N^*.

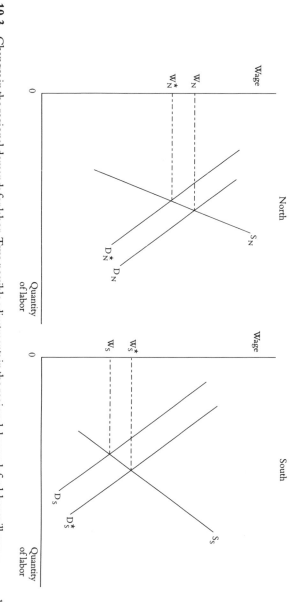

equipment to that region. This adjustment would not only increase the demand for labor in the South as before but would also decrease the demand for labor in the North to $D_N^\star$ and decrease the market wage for occupation A to $W_N^\star$.

There is a second adjustment on the demand side, an adjustment involving product price. If the average wage for occupation A is lower in the South than in the North, then, other things equal, the costs of production (and thus product prices) are lower in the South. As consumers shift their purchases away from the higher-priced output of the North toward the lower-priced output of the South, the demand for labor in the South increases to $D_S^\star$ (because of the increase in the price of southern output), thus raising the wage for occupation A in the South to $W_S^\star$. The decline in demand for northern output decreases the price of northern output, thus decreasing the demand for labor in that region to $D_N^\star$ and lowering the wage to $W_N^\star$. Thus, trade in goods across regions within a nation is another mechanism that tends to eliminate the difference in average real wages for like types of labor across regions within a nation.

Thus, economic theory does conclude that three powerful forces will move the average real wage for like types of labor toward equality across regions within a nation. Those variables are migration of labor, migration of capital, and trade in goods. Notice, however, that average real wages (and incomes) across regions will still differ because of differences in the industrial mix across regions. Nonetheless, while average real wages (and incomes) continue to differ across regions, individuals *in each occupation* will tend to earn the same average real wage in all regions within a nation in purely competitive labor markets.

Because the average real wage for any given occupation tends toward equality across regions in purely competitive labor markets, individuals in any given occupation cannot, on average, improve the real wage at which they can work by changing regions. Individuals can, however, equip themselves to enter higher-paying occupations within a region by making investments in themselves. Chapter 12 presents this human-capital investment decision. Before leaving this topic, however, it is possible to pursue this discussion one step further. By doing so you come to the boundary of an important sub-area in economics: international economics.

10.3   AVERAGE REAL WAGES FOR OCCUPATION A: EQUALITY ACROSS NATIONS?

Does economic theory predict that the average real wage for like types of labor will tend toward equality across nations? Is there any expectation, for example, that the average wage for certified public accountants with identical years of experience will tend toward equality between the United States and Mexico? Section 10.2 identified three adjustment mechanisms that bring the average wage for like types of labor into equality across regions within a nation. In the United States, the Constitution prevents states from erecting any barriers to these adjustment mechanisms. If individuals choose to migrate from Michigan to California, they are free to do so. If producers wish to relocate capital from Delaware to Texas, they are free to do so. If consumers wish to shift their purchases from the output of the Northeast to that of the Southwest, they are free to do so.

If these same adjustment mechanisms were allowed to operate across national boundaries (that is, if international markets were purely competitive), the same conclusions would follow for international comparisons that follow for comparisons within nations. However, there are barriers across nations that prevent these adjustment mechanisms from operating: immigration controls, capital controls, and import quotas, tariffs, and duties on goods and services. Nonetheless, to the degree that these adjustment mechanisms are allowed to operate, one will find a tendency for the average real wage for like types of labor to tend toward equality across nations. Courses in international economics explore these impediments to adjustment across nations and often present estimates of the loss in economic welfare resulting from barriers to adjustment.

10.4   QUESTIONS

1. How might the analysis of industrial wage differences presented in Section 10.1 be altered if workers prefer the working conditions in one industry over those of another?

2. The analysis in Section 10.1 suggests that there will be a relation between productivity growth and wage growth in an industry in the short run, but not in the long run. True or false, and explain.

3. The North American Free Trade Agreement lowers barriers to the movement of capital and goods across the member nations. How will wage differences for like types of labor be affected?

—— 11 ——

Monopsony and Rent-Seeking Activity in Labor Markets

A number of conclusions we have reached in Part II will be altered if labor markets are not purely competitive. For example, workers in imperfectly competitive labor markets will receive a wage less than their VMPP. If workers receive a wage less than their contribution to the firm's total revenue, then they are exploited. Section 11.1 explains why exploitation of labor occurs in imperfectly competitive labor markets. We also encounter "rent-seeking" activity again, and discover how workers may be prevented from entering higher-paying occupations even though they are willing to undertake the human-capital investment necessary to do so.

11.1 MONOPSONY

The purely competitive model presented in Chapter 7 incorporated a set of assumptions. First, there are enough firms so that the actions of any one firm do not affect the market demand for labor and therefore the wage rate. In this model, all firms take the market wage as given. Second, no firm has any preference for one worker over another. To the firm, all labor inputs are perfect substitutes for each other. Third, no artificial barriers constrain the entry of workers into the various occupations. When combined, these three assumptions are sufficient to generate a limit-case model of the labor market, a market in which all workers are confronted with the widest conceivable array of options in employment.

But there is another limit-case model: monopsony. In this model, workers confront the smallest conceivable array of options in employment. Not surprisingly, workers become worse off in identifiable ways as a result of the limitations on their employment opportunities.

143

The Monopsony Model   The essential characteristics of the monopsony model can be best understood by comparing it to the purely competitive model. Figure 11.1 replicates the model of pure competition in the labor market. (See Figure 7.4 and its discussion to review this model.) The market demand for labor (D) and the market supply of labor (S) in Figure 11.1 (a) generate an equilibrium wage W_E and an equilibrium volume of employment Q_E. The profit-maximizing firm in Figure 11.1 (b) chooses to employ q workers at wage W. What happens to this firm if it becomes a monopsonist?

The monopsonist is the one buyer of labor. If the firm in Figure 11.1 (b) becomes a monopsonist, then the market supply of labor (S) in Figure 11.1 (a) becomes the supply of labor to the one buyer of labor. Thus, in the model of monopsony represented in Figure 11.2, the supply of labor to the monopsonist (S) is upward-sloping, indicating that the monopsonist will have to raise the wage in order to attract additional workers.

If in purely competitive labor markets the firm can hire all the labor it chooses to at the market wage of, say, $20.00, then the addition to the firm's total costs from hiring an additional worker (MFC) is $20.00, an amount equal to the wage. Notice in Figure 11.2, however, that for the monopsonist, the MFC for any quantity of labor is greater than the wage at which that quantity of labor can be hired. Why is MFC greater than the wage for the monopsonist? Keep in mind that labor supply is a series of "if, then" statements. Thus, for example, *if* the wage were $20.00, *then* 10 workers would be available at that wage. *If*, alternatively, the wage were $22.00, *then* 11 workers would be available to the firm. Because this is the case, is $22.00 the MFC of the 11th worker? The firm's total costs increase from $200 to $242 by hiring 11 instead of 10 workers. MFC for the 11th worker, then, is not $22.00, the wage at which 11 workers are available. MFC of the 11th worker is $42.00, the amount by which the firm's total costs change from hiring 11 workers rather than 10.

Given a schedule indicating how the firm's total costs increase from hiring additional inputs of labor, and given as well a schedule of those workers' VMPP, the profit-maximizing monopsonist chooses to employ Q workers, that quantity for which VMPP = MFC. The monopsonist, however, has a second decision to make. Because there is no market-determined wage, it must choose how much to pay Q workers. It chooses to pay the wage W, a wage equal to the minimum wage that Q workers are willing to work. (The supply schedule indicates the minimum wages at which various quantities of labor are willing to work.)

Workers employed in purely competitive labor markets receive a wage equal to the VMPP of the last worker hired. Note this result in Figure 11.1 (b)

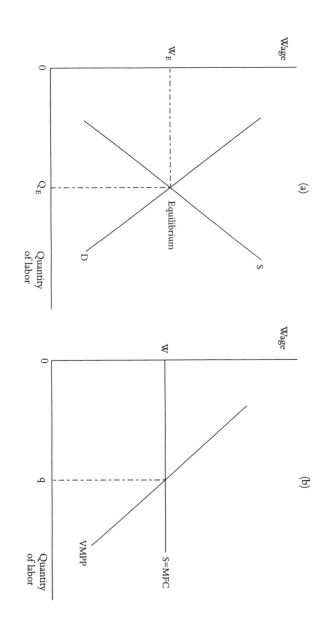

Figure 11.1 Pure competition in the labor market. The market demand for labor and the market supply of labor in panel (a) establish an equilibrium wage W_E. At that wage, the supply of labor to the firm in panel (b) is perfectly elastic. If this firm becomes a monopsonist, then the market supply of labor (S) becomes the supply of labor to the firm.

where the wage W is equal to the VMPP of the qth worker. By contrast, workers in monopsonistic labor markets receive a wage (W) that is less than the VMPP of the last worker hired. Thus, workers in monopsonistic labor markets are exploited. The concept of exploitation has nothing to do with whether the wage is high or low. Workers may earn low wages due to low amounts of embodied human capital. If workers receive low wages but those wages are equal to their VMPP, then workers are not exploited. Exploitation means only that a worker receives a wage less than the VMPP of the last worker hired.

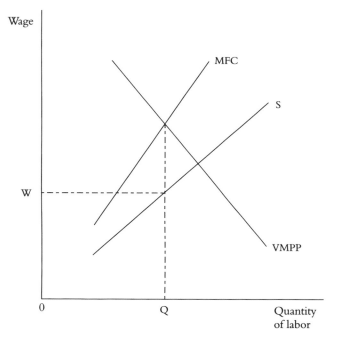

Figure 11.2 The monopsony model. If the firm is the one buyer of labor in a market, then the market supply of labor is the supply of labor to the firm. The rising supply schedule of labor to the firm illustrates that additional quantities of labor are available to the firm, but only at higher wages. Because the higher wages necessary to attract additional workers must be paid all workers, the schedule that illustrates how the firm's total costs change by hiring additional workers (MFC) lies above the supply schedule, and increases at a faster rate. The profit-maximizing monopsonist hires Q workers, that quantity for which VMPP = MFC. For that quantity, the firm pays W, the minimum wage at which that quantity of labor is available. In the model of monopsony, workers are exploited. This is because the wage (W) at which workers are employed is less than the VMPP of labor.

Also note that there is excess demand for labor (not illustrated) at wage W. Thus, one indication of monopsony in labor markets is the existence of chronic unfilled vacancies in those markets. Although there are chronic unfilled vacancies at that wage, there is no incentive for the monopsonist to raise wages to eliminate the shortage. The combination of wages and employment that the monopsonist has chosen is that combination that maximizes profits.

In both the monopsony model and the purely competitive model, self-interest-seeking individuals are pursuing their own objectives by means of exchange. Where this model differs from the purely competitive model is in the number of options in exchange. In the purely competitive model economists construct the widest conceivable array of options in employment for an individual: all those employers who employ workers in his occupation. By contrast, the monopsony model is a construction that deliberately confronts workers with the smallest conceivable number of options in employment: one employer. Not surprisingly, workers become worse off given a narrowing of their options in employment.

11.2 RENT-SEEKING ACTIVITY IN LABOR MARKETS

In Chapter 6, we first encountered the concept of rent-seeking activity. There we discovered that it is in the interest of existing producers in any industry to block the entry of new firms into their industry. Doing so stops the long-run movement of product price toward minimum LRATC, thus protecting their profits. Rent-seeking activity in the product market is the name that economists give to all activity directed toward blocking or thwarting the entry of new firms into an industry. In this section, we discover that individuals also engage in rent-seeking activity in the labor market. A discussion of this activity in the labor market begins with an expanded presentation of the concept of rent.

Pure Rent In order to present the concept of pure rent, it is helpful first to define a factor of production in such a way that its long-run supply is perfectly inelastic. Because it does not matter at this point what this factor of production is called, call it factor X. Figure 11.3 illustrates a perfectly inelastic long-run supply of this factor (S). Given the supply of X and the market demand for X (D), an equilibrium price (R_E) and quantity (Q_E) of it are determined. Now let the market demand for X increase to D^*. The first and *only* effect of this increase in market demand is to raise the equilibrium price of X to R_E^*. The rise in the price of X does not lead to any increase in the short-run supply of X. Because there are no such adjustments possible in the supply of X, there is no tendency for R_E^* to decline because of any supply increases. Thus, the rise in the equilibrium price of X to R_E^* marks the end of the story.

All factors of production have one common characteristic: they are all productive. If more of any one of them is employed in a production process, output increases. Although factors of production do have this central common characteristic, it is nonetheless possible to distinguish among them in important analytical ways. What is this factor of production X, the supply of which is perfectly inelastic even in the long run? This factor of production is land. By land, economists do not mean any particular type of land (such as land for housing developments, agriculture, industrial use, or recreation). As defined by the noted English economist David Ricardo, "land" refers to the

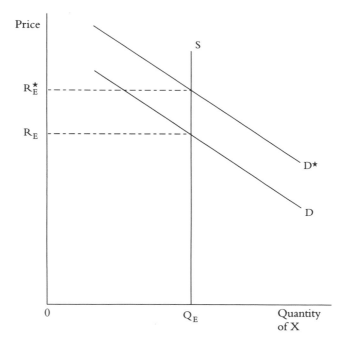

Figure 11.3 Pure rent. The market demand for land (D) and the market supply of land (S) establish an equilibrium rent, R_E. An increase in the demand for land to D^* raises rent to R_E^*. Because the long-run supply of land is perfectly inelastic, no increases in its quantity will be forthcoming in the long run in response to its higher price. Thus, there will be no increases in supply to erode R_E^* in the long run. Thus, a pure rent is a price that exhibits no tendency to erode because of any supply increases.

inherent and indestructible powers of the soil. What purpose is served by defining a factor of production in such an abstract way? The answer, of course, is to generate a price that exhibits no tendency to erode over time because of any supply increases. The only factor price that exhibits no tendency to decline over time because of an increase in market supply is pure rent. Thus, R_E^* in Figure 11.3 is pure rent.

There are, however, some factors of production whose supply characteristics in the short run resemble the supply characteristics of land in the long run. The supply of some highly skilled occupations, for example, is highly inelastic in the short run. Any increase in the demand for such an occupation will generate an element of rent in that occupational wage, but that rent will not be permanent. Thus, that rent will not be a pure rent but a quasi-rent.

Quasi-Rents in the Labor Market   In order to encounter rents in the labor market, first define the long-run supply of labor to some highly skilled occupation. Figure 11.4 illustrates the long-run supply of dentists. Like any other supply schedule, this schedule illustrates a series of "if, then" statements. However, in this case, the wage is not an absolute wage but a relative wage, W_D/W_E, the wage of dentists, W_D, relative to some index of wages of other physicians or other professionals, W_E. Thus, if the wage ratio were 1.30 (that is, if dentists earned 30 percent more than an index of wages of other physicians), then the quantity supplied of dentists in the long run would be Q. If, on the other hand, the wage ratio rose to 1.40, then the quantity supplied of dentists in the long run would increase to Q^*.

Alternatively, the long-run supply of dentists (S_{LR}) can be interpreted another way that is equally correct. This schedule illustrates the minimum wage difference necessary to induce various quantities of individuals to become dentists in the long run. Thus, in order to induce the quantity Q individuals to become dentists in the long run, a minimum wage ratio of 1.30 must be paid. To increase the long-run quantity of dentists to Q^*, a rise in minimum wage ratio to 1.40 is necessary.

Figure 11.5 illustrates a long-run equilibrium relative wage and quantity for dentists. The market demand for dentists (D) in combination with the long-run supply of dentists (S_{LR}) has generated a long-run relative wage of dentists of 1.30 and a long-run quantity of dentists of Q_E. The actual wage ratio (1.30) is the minimum necessary to induce the quantity Q_E of dentists in the long run. Now, disturb this equilibrium by increasing the market demand for dentists to D^*, and observe the adjustments toward a new equilibrium.

In addition to the long-run supply of dentists, there is a short-run supply. In Figure 11.5, S' is the initial short-run supply. The increase in the demand for dentists to D* does produce some adjustments in quantities supplied in the short run, because the increase in market demand creates an excess demand for dentists at the wage ratio 1.30. The relative wage of dentists rises immediately to 1.60. At that higher wage ratio, there is a short-run increase in the quantity supplied of dentists to Q′ (a movement along the short-run supply schedule, S′). These short-run adjustments are possible because some dentists who are currently employed will increase hours worked at the more attractive wage ratio, and some dentists who have recently retired might choose to re-enter the labor force to resume work at this higher wage ratio.

This wage ratio and short-run quantity are not equilibrium combinations, however. The minimum wage difference necessary to attract the quantity Q′ to dentistry in the long-run is only 1.35, and the new wage ratio of 1.60 is

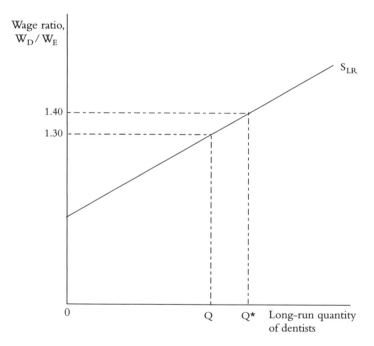

Figure 11.4 The long-run supply of dentists. The quantity of dentists available to an economy in the long-run varies directly with the wage rate of dentists (W_D) relative to wages in other relevant occupations (W_E): W_D/W_E. If the wage ratio were 1.30, then the long-run quantity of dentists available would be Q. If the wage ratio rose to 1.40, then the long-run quantity of dentists would increase to Q*. Alternatively, 1.30 is the minimum wage difference necessary to attract Q dentists in the long-run. In order to attract Q* dentists in the long run, the wage ratio must rise to 1.40.

well in excess of that. The wage ratio 1.60 attracts more individuals into dental school. After these new entrants have graduated and entered the labor market, the short-run supply of dentists increases to S″. This is an equilibrating adjustment. The effect of the increase in short-run supply of dentists is to generate a new equilibrium combination of wage ratios and employment in the labor market for dentists. The wage ratio 1.45 is an equilibrium wage ratio, for a wage ratio of 1.45 is necessary to induce the quantity Q_E'' into dentistry in the long run.

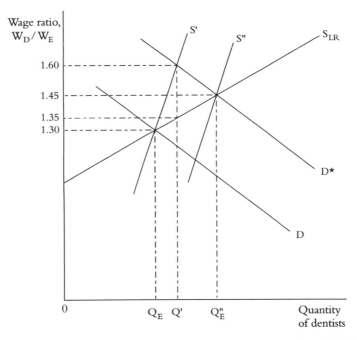

Figure 11.5 Rent seeking in the market for dentists. This market is initially in equilibrium with a wage ratio of 1.30 and Q_E dentists employed. Given the short-run supply of dentists (S′), an increase in the demand for dentists to D★ initially raises the wage ratio to 1.60. At this higher wage ratio, there is an increase in quantity supplied of dentists to Q′, even in the short run. But because 1.60 is a wage ratio well in excess of the minimum necessary to attract this quantity of dentists in the long run, the short-run supply of dentists increases to S″. Thus, the overpayment of dentists is a short-run phenomenon (a quasi-rent) that disappears as the wage ratio becomes 1.45, the minimum necessary to attract Q_E'' dentists in the long run. If, however, dentists can block the supply increase, then they can transform the wage ratio 1.60 into a permanent phenomenon (a pure rent).

The wage ratios of 1.30 and 1.45 are both equilibrium wage ratios, because they represent the minimum wage differences necessary to induce the quantities Q_E and Q_E'' respectively, into dentistry in the long run. The wage ratio 1.60 is not an equilibrium wage ratio, however, for that actual wage ratio is greater than the minimum necessary to induce the quantity Q' into dentistry in the long run. That necessary minimum wage ratio is only 1.35. The difference between 1.35 and 1.60 represents a short-run overpayment of dentists. It is an element of rent in dentists' wages.

Notice, however, that this short-run overpayment of dentists is not permanent. The increase in the short-run supply to S" eliminates this rent. Thus, this overpayment is not a pure rent; pure rents do not get eroded or eliminated because of any supply increases. This overpayment is a rent but is not a pure rent; it is a quasi-rent, "almost" a pure rent. It is a temporary phenomenon that occurs in labor markets due to the fact that adjustments to change in labor markets do not occur instantaneously or without costs. Quasi-rents, then, are characteristics of labor markets in purely competitive markets.

Rent Seeking in Labor Markets   It is possible to transform what otherwise would be a temporary feature of a labor market into a permanent feature. The quasi-rent created in Figure 11.5 disappears as the short-run supply of labor increases to S". By preventing the supply increase, this quasi-rent can be transformed into a pure rent. Rent-seeking activity, then, is all activity designed to block (or impede) the increase in the supply of labor to this occupation.

Many occupational associations engage in successful rent-seeking activity that perpetuates an element of rent in their occupational wage. Take physicians and the American Medical Association (AMA). The AMA is able to regulate the supply of physicians because it accredits medical schools. This successful example of rent-seeking activity has costs to the larger society, however. The health of the population is increased by all sorts of things that people do for themselves (watching their weight, getting enough exercise, and not smoking, for example). But their health is also increased by professional services that physicians perform for their patients. To the extent that rent-seeking activity by the AMA is successful, it limits the supply of physicians. To the extent that the supply of physicians is limited, the stock of health of the population is less than it otherwise would be. Thus, the gain in physician wages (and thus income) comes at the expense of the health of the population. Furthermore, among the population, the least advantaged members are the most seriously impacted.

Other occupational associations perform the same type of rent-seeking activities for their members. Craft unions are particularly successful in controlling membership in their unions, thus maintaining noncompetitive wages that may contain substantial amounts of rent. Veterinarians are successful in restricting interstate mobility through licensing requirements of one type or another. Hair stylists impose their own kind of supply blockage by requiring hundreds of hours of formal training to cut hair. All these examples of rent-seeking activity benefit the existing members of an occupation at the expense of new entrants into the occupation and the public at large. In addition, all of this activity has a clear implication for the distribution of money income across households.

11.3 RENTS AND THE DISTRIBUTION OF INCOME ACROSS HOUSEHOLDS

The wage at which household members can work is determined in large part by the amount of their embodied human capital. Thus, a substantial portion of the actual difference in money incomes across households can be explained by differences in the educational attainment and years of on-the-job training of household members. But some portion of the actual income differences across households is due to an element of rent in occupational wages. Because rent is likely to appear more frequently in higher rather than in lower average wages, rent in occupational wages tends to shift the distribution of money income toward higher income households.

11.4 QUESTIONS

1. The market for nurses is typically cited as an occupational labor market that exhibits chronic (period after period) unfilled job vacancies. Is there a chronic shortage of nurses? If so, do you think these chronic unfilled vacancies are due to monopsony power? Explain.
2. Is it possible that a major league athlete who earns $1,200,000 a year is exploited?
3. The wages of unionized electricians in New York City contain a huge element of rent. Because membership into the union is carefully regulated, what factor best predicts who is admitted into the union when openings do occur?
4. Even if labor markets were purely competitive, many occupational wages would contain an element of rent. True or false, and explain.

——12——

Human Capital

The maximum wage that a profit-maximizing firm will be willing to pay a worker is the VMPP of that worker, the amount by which the firm's total revenue increases by hiring the worker. Thus, workers can increase the wage at which they can work by becoming more productive. Firms can make their workers more productive by making human-capital investments in them, but individuals can also make themselves more productive by making human-capital investments in themselves. What exactly is a human-capital investment in an individual?

12.1 THE CONCEPTS OF CAPITAL AND INVESTMENT

Any discussion of investment requires a simultaneous discussion of the concept of capital because these two concepts are necessarily linked.

Capital A common definition of capital is "a stock of produced means of production." This definition contains three distinguishing characteristics of capital. First, capital is a stock, not a flow. Second, capital is a stock of means of production. But some means of production are given and some are produced; the common definition of capital takes this into account by defining a third distinguishing characteristic: capital is a produced means of production. Before applying these aspects of capital to humans, consider first a nation's capital.

The capital of the United States is the stock of produced productive capacity of the United States. The capital stock of the United States consists of the plant and equipment of the nation because plant and equipment represents productive capacity that has been produced. The stock of knowledge has been produced as well, so it is also part of the capital stock. Some portions of the productive capacity of the United States have not been

155

produced, however. The harbors and rivers of the nation, the mineral deposits, and the inherent fertility of the soil are part of the nation's productive capacity, but they were not produced – and, therefore, not capital.

Human Capital   A nation's human capital is the stock of produced productive capacity embodied in individuals. The human capital stock includes all the skills embodied in individuals because all skills are by definition acquired. Abilities are also embodied in individuals, but they are innate, not acquired. Thus, although the abilities embodied in individuals are part of their productive capacity, those abilities are not part of the individual's human capital.

Investment   A stock of produced productive capacity will, when employed, yield a flow of real output per unit time. That flow of real output will, when sold, yield a flow of income (Y) to its producers. Assume here that the flow of real income is the annual flow called Gross Domestic Product, the dollar value of all final output produced in the United States annually.

This annual flow of income can either be consumed (C) during the current time period or not consumed during the current time period. The decision not to consume income is saving (S). Thus, the first observation one can make is that a nation's annual flow of income is either consumed or not consumed: $Y = C + S$. Assume that a nation during year t consumes all of its income: $C_t/Y_t = 1$. If this occurs, will the levels of Y or C next year (in year t + 1) be affected?

Capital does not have eternal life. In the process of producing output in year t, some capital is used up. If this capital is not replaced, the flow of income in year t + 1 will be lower, thus lowering consumption in year t + 1. (Keep in mind that income is the variable that constrains consumption.) To prevent the capital stock from declining, some expenditure in year t from annual income in year t is necessary to replace the capital used up. That expenditure is replacement investment. Thus, some investment is necessary in a nation simply to prevent the capital stock from decreasing in size. Furthermore, this fact requires that saving in a nation be at least sufficient to finance replacement investment. (This discussion ignores any consideration of international movement of savings and investment.) Because saving is nonconsumption, some consumption in the present is necessarily sacrificed to have replacement investment.

Whereas replacement investment is necessary to prevent the capital stock from decreasing, additional investment is necessary to increase the size of the capital stock. Investment that increases the size of the capital stock is net investment. Because net investment increases the capital of a nation, the annual flows of income and consumption increase in future time periods. Thus, net investment is necessary in order for a nation to achieve higher future levels of consumption, and higher future consumption necessarily requires that consumption in the present be less than it could be.

Total investment in a nation is the sum of its two component parts: replacement investment plus net investment. For a nation's annual income and consumption to rise over time, annual saving must be sufficient to finance these two types of investment. In addition, for a nation's per-capita income and per-capita consumption to grow over time, the rate of growth of net investment must exceed the growth rate of population.

Thus far, this discussion has not conceptualized consumption. If investment is that expenditure that either replaces or adds to the produced productive capacity of a nation, what is consumption? Consumption is an expenditure that neither replaces nor adds to produced productive capacity of a nation. It is, rather, an expenditure that individuals make guided solely by considerations of their own utility in the present. What this discussion makes evident, however, is that future income and consumption will decline if nations consume in the present all that it is possible for them to consume.

Human-Capital Investment   All individuals have some amount of embodied human capital that, when employed, yields a flow of income per unit time. Because human capital does not have eternal life, some skills erode or become obsolete over time. In order to prevent one's human-capital stock from declining, some replacement investment is necessary – investment that replaces human capital worn out in the process of producing annual income. Thus, some consumption must necessarily be sacrificed in the present in order to finance replacement investment. (If, for example, you choose to delay entry into a new job in your given occupation for three months in order to re-tool some skills, you sacrifice the consumption you could have achieved had you worked rather than gone to school.)

Different occupations require different skills. If you are currently employed in occupation A but desire to move to occupation B where the wage is higher, you will normally be required to make net investment in your human capital. Net investment in human capital is an expenditure that increases your stock of human capital and thus enables you to enter the higher-wage occupation.

12.2   HUMAN-CAPITAL INVESTMENTS THAT FIRMS MAKE IN WORKERS

Firms routinely make investments in their workers. Why would a firm assumed to maximize profits incur the costs of making investments in its workers?

Why Does a Firm Invest in Its Workers?   Firms make human-capital investments in their workers in the form of on-the-job training (OJT). One piece of information that a profit-maximizing firm will consider in this decision is how its total revenues will increase by doing so. An individual worker employed in a firm is currently adding to the firm's total revenues with his given skills. That measure is his VMPP. Would his VMPP increase if he received OJT? Because an investment in the human capital of workers makes them more productive, his MPP would rise, thus raising his VMPP. This increase in VMPP is the benefit to the firm from providing OJT to the worker. Furthermore, this benefit is not only in the present; his VMPP in future time periods will be higher as well. During the lifetime of the investment, his VMPP with OJT will be higher than it would have been without OJT. It is possible through the process of discounting to estimate the present value of these future differences in his VMPP. It is this present value of future differences in VMPP that a profit-maximizing producer compares to the present costs of providing the training.

The present costs of providing OJT to workers are varied. These costs may include the wages of instructors or others conducting the training, any lost output that results from removing the worker from production in order to undergo the training, any materials used in the training process, and any other expenses associated with raising the MPP of the worker.

A firm will choose to provide OJT to a particular worker if the present value of the benefits of OJT exceed the present value of the costs. When a firm has to ration OJT among its employees, it will choose to provide the training to those workers who have the highest ratio of benefits to costs. There may be some variation across workers in the costs of providing training. The variation across workers in the benefits of the training are likely to be much more substantial, however. The present value of future differences in VMPP will be greater for younger rather than older workers because younger workers have more years of potential work with the firm. The present value of future VMPP differences will also be greater, on average, for men than for women because women are more likely to have an interrupted work experience as they withdraw from the labor force to have and raise children.

What Sort of Training Do Firms Provide?   Consider specific investment first. Training that is perfectly firm-specific raises the VMPP of the worker only in the firm providing the training. It is rare that any training is quite this specific, but there is training that raises the VMPP of a worker in one industry only. Assume that a worker's VMPP is $12 an hour without OJT but rises to $14 after specific training. The benefit to the firm from providing the training is the present value of the additional $2 in revenues over the lifetime of the investment. A firm will be willing to incur the costs of providing this specific training because this worker cannot employ this training in alternative employments. Thus, as long as the firm pays this worker more than $12 an hour (his VMPP without OJT), there is no incentive for him to leave this firm and employ his skills elsewhere.

By contrast, perfectly general investment is training that increases the VMPP of a worker in the widest possible array of alternative employments. Reading, writing, and computational skills are perfectly general skills that workers use in every occupation. What if in the preceding example the worker's VMPP had increased from $12 to $14 because the firm made an investment in general training? Because general training increases the VMPP of workers in virtually all employments, other firms (who have not incurred the costs of training) would be willing to hire this worker and pay him $14 an hour (his VMPP). In this instance, the firm providing the training would lose all of the investment it had made in this worker. Thus, firms will be reluctant to incur the costs of providing general training to their workers.

Labor Hoarding   Assume that there is a decline in the demand for a firm's output. The firm chooses to reduce output and does so initially by reducing hours worked by existing employees. If the decline in demand is thought to be permanent, however, the firm begins to lay off workers. The workers laid off first will tend to be those in whom the firm has made the least investments in OJT. This is the low-cost choice because firms have minimal investments in these workers and they will be easy to replace in the event of an upturn in sales. By contrast, firms will hoard workers in whom they have made substantial investments. Not only would they lose the investment they have made in these workers, they would have to remake that investment with new workers in the future. This phenomenon suggests that cyclical variations in the unemployment rate will be less for skilled workers than for unskilled workers.

12.3   HUMAN-CAPITAL INVESTMENTS THAT INDIVIDUALS MAKE IN THEMSELVES

Individuals, of course, also make human capital investments in themselves. The first example that comes to your mind is probably the educational investments that people make. But the human-capital framework also allows an analysis of other types of investments that people make in themselves, investments such as migration and investments in their health. Before considering some investments that individuals make in themselves, it is important to establish the rationale for this investment decision.

Utility and Present-versus-Future Consumption   The present cost to an individual of making a human-capital investment is necessarily less consumption (and thus less utility) in the present. Within the context of a model of utility maximization, why would any individual ever choose less consumption in the present? The answer, of course, is because sacrificed consumption transformed into human-capital investment in the present is expected to make higher consumption (and thus higher utility) possible in the future. Thus, the benefit to an individual of this investment is the present value of the higher expected consumption and utility in the future made possible by the investment. Thus, within a utility-maximizing framework, an individual is comparing less consumption and utility today to more consumption and more utility in the future.

This present-versus-future decision requires noting one particularly important way in which individuals differ from each other: the rate at which they are willing to sacrifice present for future consumption. This rate has a particular name in economics: an internal rate of time preference. By *internal* we mean that it is a subjective characteristic of individuals. Thus, it is akin to a taste and preference variable, not a characteristic of the environment. In addition, this rate is always positive. No individual would willingly sacrifice one ice cream cone today for one ice cream cone tomorrow. Because of uncertainty, individuals require more consumption tomorrow to induce them to sacrifice consumption today. But, having said that, individuals will differ in their rate. If an individual is willing to give up consumption in the present only if he can attain 15 percent more in the future, then he has a 15 percent internal rate of time preference. Another individual with a higher internal rate of time preference may be willing to give up consumption in the present only if he can attain 18 percent more in the future.

If an individual has an internal rate of time preference of 11 percent, he will be willing to borrow the savings to make the investment at market rates of interest of 11 percent or less. If the market rate of interest rises above 11 percent, then he will not make this investment. A rise in the rate of interest, then, reduces the quantity of human-capital investments that individuals make in themselves.

Investments in Education, Migration, and Health   One immediate implication of the human-capital model has led to the rise of a new sub-area of economics: the economics of education. Individuals can increase their human capital by making investments in themselves, and those investments do generate higher income and consumption in the future. It makes no difference whether those investments are in university degrees or vocational training; both types of investments have the same analytical effect of increasing human capital.

Migration is also an investment that individuals can make in themselves. Chapter 10 concluded that average real wages for like types of labor tend toward equality across both industries and regions in the long run in purely competitive markets. Within an industry, however, there are differences in average wages across firms at any given time. Large firms often pay higher average wages than small firms, and urban employers commonly pay higher wages than rural employers. Thus, within any industry there may be some real wage gains possible as an individual relocates from a small, rural employer to a larger, urban employer within a given industry. Furthermore, similar real wage gains may also be possible across regions. If an individual can increase the real wage for his given skills in future time periods by relocating, the decision to relocate is a human-capital decision that is made by comparing the present value of the future gains from migration to the present costs of migration.

Expenditures that individuals make in maintaining or improving their health are also a human-capital investment. The average life expectancy in the United States and other high-income nations approaches 80. In some poor countries, average life expectancy is closer to 40. Any private investments that individuals make in improving their own health, or any public-health investments that nations make to eradicate disease or improve the nutrition of the population, increase the stream of output from the population. Of course, there are other benefits from these investments that we measure in other ways.

12.4 HUMAN CAPITAL AND THE DISTRIBUTION OF INCOME ACROSS HOUSEHOLDS

In purely competitive markets, some portion of the difference in annual labor income across households will depend on the labor supply decisions that household members make. Some individuals have relatively high annual incomes even though the wage at which they can work is not high. They are able to accomplish this by working longer-than-average hours per year. For example, many immigrant workers have higher annual incomes than native workers with the same levels of education. This difference is not attributable to higher wages for given skills, but to longer hours worked on average.

The second determinant of annual labor income is the wage at which an individual can work. Generally speaking, this wage varies directly with the amount of human capital embodied in the individual. One reason that physicians have the highest annual labor income of any occupational group in the United States is that they work longer-than-average hours each week, closer to 60 hours a week than 40. But an important portion of this high income is due to the very high wage at which they work. This high wage, in turn, is due in large part to the enormous amounts of human capital embodied in physicians.

These two variables explain equally well why some individuals earn lower-than-average annual incomes. One reason is hours worked. Surveys continue to show that roughly half the individuals who are poor in the United States work fewer than 40 hours per week, 50 weeks per year. In part, this is the result of unemployment – something that happens to an individual. But, in part, this is the result of the choice that an individual makes to work less than full-time. By contrast, the other half of the poor work full-time. They are poor because their embodied skills do not qualify them for available jobs that pay higher-than-average wages. These two realities support the widely held view among economists that maintaining high levels of aggregate employment combined with strengthened primary and secondary education are the two most important antipoverty strategies that any nation can employ.

12.5 QUESTIONS

1. If individuals consume all of their income from period to period, what happens to their income and consumption over time? Why?

2. Is there any necessary link between increased expenditures on public education and human-capital formation in students?

3. An internal rate of time preference presupposes a perception of a future. Why do some individuals not give much (if any) thought to the future?

4. If all individuals who enter high school in the United States graduated with reading, writing, and computational skills at the 12th-grade level, what differences would you expect in (a) the aggregate labor force participation rate, (b) the unemployment rate, and (c) the distribution of income?

Index